ONCE UPON A RECIPE

*Delicious, Healthy Foods
For Kids Of All Ages*

KAREN GREENE

Design by Anna Marie Heinz and Karen Greene

A PERIGEE BOOK

A NEW HOPE PRESS PRODUCTION

FOR DONOVAN & LAURA, WITH LOVE . . .

Perigee Books
are published by
The Putnam Publishing Group
200 Madison Avenue, New York, NY 10016

For quote credits and acknowledgements, see page 93.

Library of Congress Cataloging-in-Publication Data:
Greene, Karen, date.
Once upon a recipe : delicious, healthy foods for kids of all ages
/ Karen Greene ; design by Anna Marie Heinz and Karen Greene.
p.   cm.
Originally published: New Hope, Pa. : New Hope Press, 1987.
Includes bibliographical references and index.
Summary: More than fifty delicious, healthy recipes with allusions
to works of children's literature and cooking tips. Sample items :
Babar's Carob French Toast, Shakespeare's Breakfast Sandwiches,
Rumpelstiltskin's Pillow, and Bambi's Salad Bowl.
ISBN 0-399-51784-7
1. Cookery—Juvenile literature.   2. Cookery (Natural foods)—
Juvenile literature.   3. Literary cookbooks—Juvenile literature.
[1. Cookery—Natural foods.   2. Literary cookbooks.]   I. Title.
TX652.5.G72   1992   92-9666   CIP   AC
641.5′123—dc20

Book design by Anna Marie Heinz & Karen Greene
Food illustrations by Mary Wentzel
Mrs. Tiggy-winkle illustration on page 21 by Holly Snyder
Printed in the United States of America
1   2   3   4   5   6   7   8   9   10

This book is printed on acid-free paper.
∞

*"I*f you would grow great and stately,
You must try to walk sedately.
You must still be bright and quiet,
And content with simple diet:
And remain, through all bewild'ring,
Innocent and honest children.
Happy hearts and happy faces,
Happy play in grassy places—
That was how, in ancient ages,
Children grew to kings and sages."

"A Child's Garden of Verses"
by Robert Louis Stevenson

THE MENU

MORNING GLORY
The best & brightest breakfasts

◆

BUNCHES OF LUNCHES
12 o'clock & all's delicious

◆

"**A** *crust eaten in peace is better than a banquet partaken in anxiety.*"

"The Town Mouse and the Country Mouse"
by Aesop

SNACKS & SIPS

Quite delightful bites
& quick quenchers

◆

42

THE SUPPER CLUB

Dinners that are
winners

◆

56

SWEET DREAMS

Dreamy desserts &
a nightcap or two

◆

74

Each page of this cookbook was created to stir a different dream. After all, the kitchen is as likely a landscape as any for bumping into fairy godmothers, for wish fulfillment, for seeing drawer after drawer of dreams come true. One can even imagine the kitchen's many occupants coming alive late at night—utensils and muffin tins tap-dancing about, blenders and egg beaters whirring a tune, while apples in the fruit bowl croon a chorus and cupboard doors applaud the moonlit performance.

◆

No matter our age, there is an enchantment about childhood, with its tales and dreams and kindly cuisine, that comes like soft music drowning out the cares and chaos of modern life. The exhilarating charm of a child's heart, a child's effortless belief in things beyond belief, invite us all to drop our limitations at the door. To share a child's inner garden is to occasionally escape the laws of gravity.

◆

In that spirit, *Once Upon A Recipe* is intended to bring parent and child together in the kitchen, mixing and giggling and baking and imagining. Many of the recipes could easily be handled by an older child working alone. Some parents may rely on the recipes most often as a sourcebook for nutritious cooking they prepare themselves, confident that their children will actually enjoy the results. But it's a joyful, *shared* journey between parent and child that is this author's dream.

◆

There are so many true and timeless thoughts from classic children's books awaiting you on these pages, and so many tasteful food ideas, that it's rather a rare bonus that the recipes all manage a great respect for the ideals of good nutrition, as well. They're a happy alternative to the abundance of recipes for children overly dependent for taste on refined sugars, flours and fats. While a little splurging of that sort is hardly cause for alarm, it's not a basis for the best everyday eating habits, which usually tag along with us all the way to adulthood. Childhood obesity is a sad tale indeed and, unfortunately, far from an uncommon sight today.

◆

For every parent who has labored at a stove and been rewarded with a turned-up nose when they tried to peddle something wholesome, take heart. *Once Upon A Recipe* has more than 50 delicious, healthy foods purposefully disguised as nonsense. Why take your chances with Whole Wheat Pancakes when you can offer Angel Cakes with Applesauce Syrup instead? (Don't think of it as deception. Think of it as marketing.)

Hopefully, you'll soon agree that the words of Lewis Carroll quoted above suit *Once Upon A Recipe* to a tea.

While parents must decide for themselves and for their children which foods are best suited to their tastes and lifestyle, here are a few nutrition ideas in a nutshell to share with the little doubting Thomases at your table.

Twinkle, Twinkle, little tummy,
How I long for something yummy.
Up above the world I'll fly
To find the pie that's in the sky.

I'll nibble cakes as light as air
And tackle tarts of plum and pear.
I'll gobble galaxies of cream cheese
And lick popsicles till I freeze.

I'll catch a comet made of fudge.
For weeks and weeks, I will not budge.
Until I've had a million mousses,
I can't be bothered with couscouses.

But whilst I thought of gooey things
I saw a-fluttering two pink wings.
My eyes then fell on strangest fairy—
Her hat full of blueberries, knees of cherries.

Tossing hair as gold as wheat
She laughed, "You'll not survive such sweets.
Your teeth will rot, your tummy ache,
Your smooth, soft skin begin to flake."

I replied, quite full of cheek,
"This picture that you paint is bleak.
What right have you to spoil my mood
And criticize my favorite food?"

"Dear child," she chuckled, "when I see
A princess who won't eat a pea,
I try to help, for that is my mission
I'm the Delicious Witch of Good Nutrition. →

"Please do not think I mean to take
All possible pleasures off your plate.
But vats of fats and fried foods by the hour,
Sacks of sugar and white flour,

"All tend to cause a chubby form
And arteries below the norm.
Some cancers, stroke and heart disease
We've linked to faulty gourmandise.

"I don't wish to scare you, but this is a fact
There's no time like the present to clean up your act.
Here's a list I've made, I've checked it twice
Of foods that are naughty and foods that are nice.

"A knight is nice white, but breads are best brown.
Whole wheat and such grains have deserved reknown.
Brown rice, corn, oats, bulgur, barley, buckwheat
Make muffins and pilafs and pancakes complete.

"With all sweeteners, much more than a little's too much.
White sugar, especially, has lost its nutritional touch.
Try honey, maple syrup, fruit juice or molasses.
They taste great and may improve your 50-yard dashes.

"Crown the complex carbohydrate your dietary king—
That's just vegies, whole grains and beans and things.
In your diet if they command 60 percent,
You will find that your vigor is not so absent.

"Like the tortoise they run the day's race slow and steady.
You'll always have energy, always be ready.
Sugary foods bring a quick charge that's gone just as quick.
They're quite like the hare, whose tricks wouldn't stick.

"Packaged foods for the modern family are grand
But read labels carefully, choose the purest of brands.
Chemical preservatives, colors and flavors announce
(Since it's best not to eat what you can't pronounce).

"But the greatest, perhaps, of all diet no-no's,
The one causing crowds along cemetery rows,
Is our penchant, our fondness, our love, our addiction
To fats and cholesterol. (Consider eviction!)

"Leave butter and cream and the like in the dust.
Use skim milk and yogurt if you don't wish to bust.
But let's speak of the yesses—the positive things.
Let's speak of cabbages and beans with strings.

"Vegetables aren't yucky, they're not food for a wake.
Mush them in a puree, tuck them in a cake.
And since they supply exemplary nutrition,
It's best to eat your vegies of your own volition.

"Go light on the meat, heavy on fish
And you may be granted your every wish.
Put a twinkle in your eye and flowers on your table,
Then invite as many friends over as you feel you're able.

"Get going in the kitchen, and whistle while you work.
If you don't learn to laugh, you might go berserk.
Decide to be happy, to learn and share and grow
And you can be sure of reaping what you sow.

"Nourish your spirit and cut down on oil.
Try to learn to stir fry, to poach and steam and broil.
Ration your anger, try passing up the salt
And you shall be healthy, perhaps to a fault."

With that, the kitchen witch turned and vanished into air
But I realized my eating habits needed much repair.
She'd taught me that I ought to take much better care of me—
Then I wondered, had I dreamt this all, *Once Upon A Recipe?*

THE NATURAL PANTRY

There's an old Scandinavian saying that "strange food tastes best." If you find an ingredient in any of the recipes that you're a stranger to, here's where to learn more about it. Why not give it a once-over now? It's far from a complete list of healthy foods you'll want to keep on hand, but it might help illuminate some unfamiliar items in this book.

very adventurous cook must eventually trek off to the natural food store or the nutrition aisle in the supermarket. What awaits you there is not nearly so foreign as it might seem at first, at least not with a bit of help and studying up.

Many foods you find there will help you make a delicious transition from a diet full of additives, fats and hightly processed ingredients to one that's far more pure and healthy. The first thing people often wonder is why natural items cost more. There's really a very good reason.

Products without preservatives can't sit on store shelves very long, so they're made in much smaller quantities, which is a more expensive way to produce foods. Manufacturers are often small companies, and for financial reasons, can't afford to produce products in the huge quantities that the commercial food giants do. Also, natural ingredients such as pure vanilla usually cost much more for manufacturers to buy than their artificial counterparts. The distribution system serving the natural foods industry is far younger and less efficient than that serving supermarkets, adding further to the cost.

But why not think of the extra cost as a down payment on a healthier, more disease-resistant body that's full of energy—and perhaps more slim and attractive, as well?

NATURAL CONDIMENTS

You won't want to miss this aisle. It's packed with indispensable stuff. Mayonnaise, relish, catsup, pickles, mustard, you name it. Lots of taste, less (or no) sweetening, purer ingredients—a food lover's delight. Try the light-tasting safflower mayonnaise and the dark and grainy miso mustard. They're just two of the many items you'll wonder how you ever did without.

NATURAL FRUIT JUICES

Look for 100% juice, with no added sweetening. These now come in a wondrous array of flavors and colors. Don't dare let the unusual names scare you off, either. (You haven't lived until you've tried something called Hibiscus Cooler.) Many people like to dilute the juices (some supermarket juices contain only 10% real juice by comparison) by adding plain or sparkling water, usually in a 50-50 ratio. You can also buy fresh-squeezed juices in the refrigerator section at natural foods stores. They come in a great variety of flavors which are ridiculously delicious and nutritious. Try to ignore the price, if you can, since you're worth it.

NATURAL JAMS, JELLIES & CONSERVES

You'll find acres of honey-sweetened or unsweetened varieties (which are actually sweetened with fruit juice) to choose from in natural food stores today. Prepare to be amazed at how terrific an unsweetened jam can taste—the fresh fruit taste really shines. And they contain as little as 18 calories per teaspoon.

Pure Maple Syrup

This is a delicious, aromatic alternative to sugar (or even honey) in your best baked goods, though it is more costly. It adds a delicate flavor in cakes, muffins and cookies, smells heavenly and is irresistible to the tastebuds. Make sure you're buying 100% pure maple syrup. Many supermarket brands contain only 2% real syrup.

To switch a recipe from sugar to maple syrup, you can substitute ⅔ to ¾ cup for 1 cup of white sugar, and reduce the total liquids in the recipe by about ⅛ of a cup.

Maple Granules

These are dried from pure maple syrup and are handy as a direct substitute for white or brown sugar. Their flavor is pretty intoxicating in all kinds of recipes. When making baked goods, try putting the granules through your flour sifter, as they're sometimes a bit coarse.

You may have to search several natural food stores or gourmet stores to find these, so it's wise to buy in quantity. Don't hesitate to ask your favorite store to special order them for you, however.

Non-Aluminum Baking Powder

Many commercial baking powders have a high dose of sodium, and many contain aluminum compounds, as well. If you've been using them, you'll probably find natural brands preferable, as they're free of the slightly bitter aftertaste that the aluminum compounds impart. Some chefs suggest using an extra teaspoon when transposing a recipe.

Nitrate-Free Meats

You'll find an increasingly large selection of high-quality meats in natural foods stores and a few supermarkets these days. They are free of the nitrate and nitrite preservatives that are known cancer-causing agents. They may even be organically raised, which means without growth hormones or antibiotics. You'll find hamburger, chicken, bacon and many other items, as well, depending on the size of the store. Some large natural supermarkets in major cities have complete fresh meat departments. These are well worth trying.

Soy Margarine

From a caloric standpoint, butter and margarine are equals. But the saturated fat contained in butter is thought to be much more likely to clog blood vessels and produce heart disease than olive oil, margarine or polyunsaturated vegetable oils. In a blind taste test, you'd have little chance of distinguishing soy margarine from regular supermarket margarine. In fact, many supermarket brands include soybean oil. But natural food store brands are usually free of the artificial colors and preservatives that those products often contain. And natural food store soy margarines usually list "liquid soybean oil" as their first ingredient, whereas supermarket brands are more likely to be mainly "partially hydrogenated soybean oil." What this means is that they'll contain more saturated fats.

There is still some disagreement as to the healthiest source of fats in the diet—with vegetable oils, margarine and even butter (in small quantities) each having their champions.

Polyunsaturated fats, such as soybean, corn, safflower and sunflower oils, had long been thought to be the most advantageous. But the lastest findings seem to indicate that olive and peanut oil, both monounsaturates, may prove even more helpful in lowering the →

amount of cholesterol in the blood. These two oils have rather assertive flavors and are unsuitable for use in most baked goods, but perform well in many other dishes. There are those who suggest the ideal is to consume one-third of our dietary fat in each category—saturates, polyunsaturates and monounsaturates.

One thing is certain. Most of us consume far too much in the way of fats and will benefit in many ways from streamlining our recipes. The average American diet is about 40% fat, with nutrition experts suggesting that figure ought to be cut in half.

Top chefs across the country are experimenting with low-fat, delicious cuisine. You can use skim milk and buttermilk in place of cream in soups, then thicken with arrowroot or even cornstarch. Yogurt and kefir cheese replace sour cream and cream cheese nicely. Mineral water can be used to thin a butter sauce. Any time you spend experimenting with these ideas will be time well spent.

If you've been awfully good, you may want to splurge and substitute butter for margarine in some of the recipes found here. There's no question that you'll add a richness of flavor that's beyond compare. But the recipes produce delicious results using the margarine or oils specified.

Where a recipe calls simply for pure vegetable oil, you might try canola oil, another monounsaturate whose delicate flavor is compatible with any ingredient.

◆

NATURAL PEANUT BUTTER

Read labels, since many supermarket brands add extra oils, sugar (often called dextrose) and other additives to keep the natural oil from separating. If it's in a jar, the only ingredient should be peanuts and, perhaps, salt (though salt-free varieties are great). Fresh ground peanut butter is hard to beat for flavor, though, and you won't have to stir the oil back in, as with natural peanut butters in jars. (It won't have time to separate before you use it up.) Always store natural peanut butter in the fridge once opened, and put fresh-ground varieties there right away.

◆

SOY MILK

While everyone may not be ready to exchange that tall, cold glass of dairy milk for soymilk, it's quite a handy tool in cooking, where any flavor differences become negligible. Why bother? The reasons are numerous. Soymilk offers as much protein as whole cow's milk, with a third as much fat, and even that is unsaturated. Unflavored varieties are equivalent to 2% milk in fat content. Its convenient shelf life—up to six months—and lower cost are other benefits. It's a handy item to have on the shelf for those times when you want to whip something up and find you're out of dairy milk.

A 1982 article in the *Journal of the American Medical Association* suggested that merely by replacing dairy milk with soy milk, Americans could significantly reduce their risk of coronary heart disease, with recent research showing that soymilk may actually lower plasma cholesterol levels.

Flavored varieties, such as vanilla, carob malted or strawberry, can be used in countless creative ways, as well. Where soymilk is called for in *Once Upon A Recipe*, whole or lowfat milk can always be substituted.

Nutrition experts do suggest using mainly whole milk products for children under two—a few say as late as four—since the calories and protein are thought essential for proper brain development. You can easily adjust recipes accordingly, to suit your family's needs.

Soy Sauce, Shoyu And Tamari

Soy sauce, shoyu and tamari are all really soy sauces. This group of fermented soybean products are traditional Eastern condiments for many foods, especially vegetables. Unlike some supermarket soy sauces, the products labeled tamari, soy sauce and shoyu that are sold in natural and gourmet stores are naturally fermented and contain no artificial preservatives or colors. Tamari is the most expensive, as it's been aged the longest and is wheat-free. It makes an excellent dipping sauce. Shoyu has a slightly sweet, rich taste that is wonderful, although it doesn't retain its flavor as well as tamari in dishes that must cook for a long period of time.

Besides imparting great flavor, all are believed by the Chinese and Japanese to aid the digestion, promote longevity and neutralize stomach acids. They can be quite high in sodium, however. According to a top producer, Eden Foods, a teaspoon of tamari contains about 250 mg. of sodium (some brands are much higher). Table salt, by comparison, has 2280 mg. of sodium per teaspoon. You can, and should, consider purchasing low-salt varieties of soy sauces, which reduce the sodium intake to about 45 mg. per teaspoon. Check labels carefully to be sure of sodium content. Government dietary recommendations call for a safe intake of from 1,000 to 3,300 mg. of salt per day in healthy individuals.

Whole Grain Baking Mixes

Explore the aisles of your natural food store or supermarket health section and you'll find a brave new world of pancake, muffin, cake and biscuit mixes made with whole grains—and without preservatives or artificial additives. These are the heart of The Natural Pantry. They're so versatile, they seem to do everything but tap dance. They're not only quick and delicious, but help provide some of the complex carbohydrates that nutritionists now say should be the largest part of a healthy diet.

Recent research has shown an anti-cancer effect from various vitamins contained in whole grains, and the fiber in whole grains is thought to afford a similar protection. You'll find many creative suggestions for using them in *Once Upon A Recipe*.

Whole Wheat Pastry Flour

A softer flour than regular whole wheat flour, this product is ideal for any baked good you're making from scratch, since it will produce a lighter end product.

Natural Yogurt And Kefir

Too delicious to believe! Available in a great range of whole milk and lowfat flavors, natural yogurt is usually sweetened with honey, always carries the best bacteria (read all about lactobacillus and its digestive benefits sometime), and comes without artificial colors, flavors and preservatives. It's the real thing! A teaspoon or two of pure maple syrup stirred into a bowl of plain natural yogurt is an inexpensive treat for young and old alike.

While yogurt's first cousin, kefir, is not nearly as well known, it's home to the same great cultures—and nearly twice the calcium. It's thick and creamy and comes in several fruit flavors. For starters, try experimenting with it in baked goods, smoothies and summer soups. **Kefir cheese,** also found in natural food stores, is an outstanding substitute for cream cheese. It contains about half the fat, and a wonderfully tangy flavor.

Never be afraid to experiment or substitute. It's always an adventure to add or subtract ingredients you know you and your family love or don't care for to produce meals that will bring a Happy Ending to your table.

MORNING

Sleepyheads arise! Here are temptations and aromas to draw the most dedicated dreamers home from the Island of Nod. The Eldest Magician has granted us another precious piece of the Great Calendar (that's a collection of moments that is here today and gone tomorrow). In return, he asks only that we make of this day a thousand and one things.

So wash that shining morning face of yours and ask not what today will bring you—ask what *you* will bring to today. Will you build a bustling city out of blocks? Offer a cool drink to the thirsty lords and ladies of the flower garden? Throw caution to the wind and seeds to a swan? Give life to a few lines of poetry? Make your dear Mama laugh?

First, fill your tummy with marvelous foods full of energy and goodness. And as you set foot into today, think of these words by U.S. poet laureate, Richard Wilbur: "Outside the open window the morning air is all awash with angels."

GLORY

ANGEL CAKES
WITH WARM APPLESAUCE SYRUP

❧ 6-8 SERVINGS ❧

You can make these twice as fast by simply adding the spices to the batter from your favorite packaged whole grain pancake mix. When cooked, cut the pancakes with an angel cookie cutter. The odds and ends can be saved to sprinkle over ice cream tonight. Or to feed any hungry fairies hanging about.

PREP TIME: 10 minutes
COOKING TIME: 15-20 minutes

2	eggs
1½	cups lowfat milk
3	tablespoons vegetable oil
1½	cups whole wheat pastry flour
¼	teaspoon salt
2	teaspoons non-aluminum baking powder*
½	teaspoon cinnamon
½	teaspoon ground ginger
	soy margarine for frying
1	cup pure maple syrup
1	cup unsweetened applesauce

1. Beat eggs well, then beat in all but the last three ingredients, one at a time.

2. Melt a pat of margarine in a frying pan over medium-low heat. Pour in batter and cook pancakes as you normally would.

3. When pancakes are done, place on a cutting board. Cut each one with an angel cookie cutter and serve immediately with Applesauce Syrup.

Applesauce Syrup: to 1 cup of warmed pure maple syrup add 1 cup unsweetened applesauce. Stir until sauce is well-blended and warm.

*available in gourmet and natural food stores

> **"T**he moment you doubt whether you can fly, you cease forever to be able to do it. The reason birds can fly and we can't is simply that they have perfect faith, for to have faith is to have wings."
> **"The Little White Bird" by J. M. Barrie**

Best Friend's Brunch

ANGEL CAKES WITH APPLESAUCE SYRUP
◆
FRESH FRUIT SALAD SERVED IN HOLLOWED ORANGE HALVES
◆
OVER THE RAINBOW MILK
◆

A delicious ending to a slumber party for twelve or even just two.

A Little Hint

Whole-grain pancakes freeze beautifully. Make a batch up on a lazy weekend morning, then pop several (enough for one serving) into a small plastic bag and freeze.

To use, thaw before popping into the toaster or toaster oven. No time to thaw? Just toast twice.

SHAKESPEARE'S BREAKFAST SANDWICHES

ᕯᔚ 4 SERVINGS ᕮᕽ

"The cowslips tall her pensioners be. In their gold coats spots you see: Those be rubies, fairy favours."

"A Midsummer-Night's Dream"
by William Shakespeare

These egg salad sandwiches with chopped bacon are as sunny and golden yellow as cowslips, the English primroses that Shakespeare made famous as the "pensioners," or guards, of the Queen of the Fairies, Titania. The bits of red pepper mimic the "rubies." You might even say that these sandwiches are A Midsummer Morn's Dream. They do make a nicely different menu. You can boil the eggs the night before, or prepare the whole egg salad ahead.

PREP TIME: 15 minutes

6 hard-cooked eggs, peeled and chopped
1 scallion, chopped
½ sweet red pepper, chopped finely
6 oz. nitrate-free bacon,* cooked, drained and chopped
¼ cup natural mayonnaise
¼ cup plain lowfat yogurt
salt and pepper, a pinch of each
2 whole grain pitas, cut in half

1. Carefully combine all but the last ingredient. Spoon into the pita halves (lined with a frilly lettuce like red leaf, if you like). Sprinkle with a bit of fresh parsley, especially if Peter Rabbit is joining you for breakfast.

*available in natural food stores

BABAR'S CAROB FRENCH TOAST
WITH ORANGE-YOGURT SAUCE

5 SERVINGS

Like Babar, once you taste this, you'll never forget how good it is. It's quickly made with packaged carob soymilk from the natural foods store. You'll find that soymilk can be used in place of milk in many a recipe, with great results. (It's handy for reducing fat and cholesterol.) If you don't have any carob soymilk, or wish to use lowfat milk, simply add 1 teaspoon of carob powder to a bit of milk or plain soymilk, making a paste, then stir in the rest of the milk.

PREP TIME: 10 minutes
COOKING TIME: 15-20 minutes

French Toast:
- 4 eggs
- ⅔ cup carob soymilk (one small package)
- ½ teaspoon vanilla
- 10 slices whole grain bread
    pinch of cinnamon
    unsweetened carob chips (optional)

Sauce:
- 2 tablespoons frozen orange juice concentrate
- 1 cup lowfat plain yogurt

1. Beat eggs in a large, shallow bowl, then add milk and vanilla. Melt a teaspoon of soy margarine in a large skillet over medium heat.

2. Dunk a slice of bread in the batter, covering both sides well. Brown the bread on one side in your pan. Flip and sprinkle with a dash of cinnamon while second side is cooking. (If you want an extra bit of sweetness, you can sprinkle a half teaspoon of maple syrup granules on each slice at this point, too.) Remove from pan when bottom is brown.

3. Top each serving with Orange Yogurt Sauce and a sprinkling of carob chips, if you like.

Orange Yogurt Sauce: Add 2 tablespoons of frozen orange juice concentrate to 1 cup lowfat yogurt and stir well.

GOODBYE, MR. (CHOCOLATE) CHIPS

More and more kids are switching to carob from chocolate. There are some good reasons. Carob, which is produced by grinding and roasting the pod of the Mediterranean locust tree, contains no caffeine or sugar (which chocolate does). It also has a fat content of just 2% (chocolate is 52% fat).

Carob is available in a powdered form, which can be substituted equally for cocoa, although carob is naturally sweet, so you can often reduce the sugar in any recipe. Carob chips, of course, can be substituted equally for chocolate chips—and they even come in wonderful flavors today, such as mint. Some carob chips are sweetened as well, often with date sugar, but if you want to control the amount of sweetening in your food, buy the unsweetened carob chips and add your sweetener of choice to a recipe. Remember again that carob, unlike chocolate, has a natural sweetness to it already. To replace 1 square of baker's chocolate in a recipe, use 3 tablespoons of carob powder mixed with 1 tablespoon of water and 1 tablespoon of vegetable oil.

You'll find soymilk flavored with carob and other flavors in natural food stores, as well. It's great heated, like chocolate milk, or used in recipes such as our French toast.

BABY BEAR'S PORRIDGE

✤ 3 SERVINGS ✤

Raisin-rich oatmeal really is "just right" with a paw's worth of peanut butter and honey on it.

PREP TIME: 5 minutes
COOKING TIME: 10 minutes

- 2 **cups water**
- 1 **cup rolled oats**
- ⅓ **cup raisins**
- 4 **teaspoons peanut butter**
- 4 **teaspoons honey**

1. Put water on to boil. When it's doing so briskly, sprinkle the oatmeal and raisins into it, stirring well. As soon as porridge begins to thicken (about 1 minute), reduce heat and simmer for about 10 minutes, stirring now and then.
2. Pour into bowls and add one teaspoon of peanut butter and honey to each. Stir well. Make a face with a few raisins on top.

A Little Hint
When measuring sticky stuff like honey or peanut butter, first coat your spoon or cup with a wee bit of oil, and they will slide out easily.

A Little Hint

Adding several tablespoons of lowfat yogurt to any whole grain baking mix will produce a moister texture in the finished product. You can use the plain variety or experiment with flavors. Blueberry yogurt in banana muffin mix, strawberry in carrot muffin mix, peach in buckwheat pancake mix, etc. It will add a wonderful hint of flavor. Never be afraid to add a bit of adventure to your cooking!

"Then Mrs. Tiggy-winkle made tea—a cup for herself and a cup for Lucie. They sat before the fire on a bench and looked sideways at one another. Mrs. Tiggy-winkle's hand holding the tea-cup was very brown, and very very wrinkly with the soap-suds; and all through her gown and her cap, there were hair-pins sticking wrong end out, so that Lucie didn't like to sit too near her."

"The Tale of Mrs. Tiggy-winkle" by Beatrix Potter

MRS. TIGGY-WINKLE'S PINEAPPLE RIGHT-SIDE-UP MUFFINS

12 MUFFINS

The prickly little washerwoman made famous by Beatrix Potter has a weakness for pineapple, and a propensity for bran muffins, so she concocted this fiber-happy recipe that combines them both. But dear Mrs. Tiggy-winkle always had that huge stack of ironing on her mind, and never remembered to make them the usual way, which is upside-down. She discovered that they were every bit as delicious, anyhow.

PREP TIME: 10 minutes
BAKING TIME: 30 minutes

> 1 **package whole grain bran muffin mix, prepared according to directions, adding 4 tablespoons lowfat natural yogurt, either plain or a favorite flavor like blueberry or raspberry, to batter**
> 4 **tablespoons pure maple syrup or maple granules**
> 6 **oz. chopped, drained pineapple (either fresh or canned, packed in natural juice)**
> **walnuts, finely chopped (optional)**

1. Preheat oven to 350° and coat muffin tin with vegetable oil.
2. Prepare mix according to directions, adding the yogurt to the batter. Fill tins ¾ full with batter. Top with pineapple, then nuts. Top with a scant teaspoon of maple syrup or granules and bake for 30 minutes.
3. When baked, run a sharp knife around each muffin and turn out while still hot.

FRUITS OF THE MORNING

The fruits of the earth bring us a bounty of health, bursting as they are with fiber, vitamins and minerals. Here are a few fruity ways to start the day.

Drizzle orange juice, a bit of honey and a dash of cinnamon on a grapefruit half, then place under the broiler for just a minute.

Drizzle Honey Lemonade (see page 69) on a banana sliced lengthwise, then bake for a few minutes.

Toss orange sections or chunks of your favorite melon with maple or vanilla yogurt.

Toss melon pieces or orange sections with Honey Lemonade and fresh chopped mint.

Toss sliced bananas and strawberries with some fresh apple cider.

Drizzle a seeded canteloupe half with Honey Lemonade and fill with favorite berries.

HUNCA MUNCA'S FRESH SQUEEZED MUFFINS

24 TINY MUFFINS

That resourceful mate of Tom Thumb's—from Beatrix Potter's "Tale of Two Bad Mice"—treats each early visitor to her little abode to these luscious miniature Orange Juice Muffins. Could this be one reason she has more guests than she can count? With whole grain biscuit mix purchased from the natural food store, you won't have to spend all day over the mixing bowl. If you want to make regular-size muffins, simply increase baking time about 5 minutes.

PREP TIME: 10 minutes
BAKING TIME: 15-20 minutes

1½ cups whole grain biscuit or baking mix
½ cup maple granules*
¼ cup melted soy margarine or vegetable oil
1 egg, lightly beaten
½ cup fresh-squeezed orange juice (about 1 medium orange
2 tablespoons plain lowfat yogurt
1 tablespoon grated orange peel

1. Preheat oven to 350°. Coat miniature muffin tin with vegetable oil.
2. Take the orange—before you squeeze the juice from it—and using a fine grater, obtain the orange peel. Gently mix first six ingredients. Add peel to batter, taking care not to overmix.
3. Fill muffin cups ¾ full and bake for 15 to 20 minutes. When they're done, you may add a sprinkle more of the maple granules to the top, if you like.

*You can substitute the same amount of maple syrup for granules in any recipe. Simply decrease the liquids by a tablespoon.

*"**L**and of kind dreams, where the mountains are blue,*
Where brownies are friendly and wishes come true.
Through your green meadows they dance hand in hand—
Little odd people of Buttercup Land."

from an early Beatrix Potter rhyme

THE ZEST TO YOU EACH MORNING

The grated peels of lemons, limes, oranges and tangerines are a splendid spark for delicious foods, not just all manner of tempting breakfasty baked goods, but everything from soups to poultry stuffing to sauces to cake icings. These peels, as well as a bit of the juice inside of their fruits, are excellent salt substitutes, as you will soon see if you experiment with them. In fact, the name given to these grated rinds is wonderfully descriptive of what they add to the foods we eat—ZEST.

The flavor in the rind is quite concentrated because of the oils contained there, so use it with a light hand. Always use a spanking clean hand grater—the smallest holes possible, please—and be sure to obtain only the colored portion of the skin, as the white beneath is rather bitter. You can buy grated peel in bottles, but the fresh variety is worlds apart. Its dashing color and spunky taste are a natural delight.

THE VIRTUOUS BAKER

Baking is not a bit difficult, but to be really good at it, try cultivating these two virtues above all others: patience and gentleness. Try not to rush. That doesn't mean it has to take all day—it simply means being organized. Have all your refrigerated ingredients warmed to room temperature. Measure carefully. Mix gently.

And try not to worry about whether your whole grain baked goods will be quite as high or as light as the ones you made with white flour and sugar. Think, instead, about their delightful nuttiness and depth of flavor. Their goodness will be with you and your guests long after the last morsel has disappeared.

You can always make your own biscuit or baking mix from scratch, if you have an extra few minutes. The following recipe makes 2 cups of **Best Homemade Biscuit Mix:** Combine ¼ teaspoon salt, 1 tablespoon non-aluminum baking powder, 1 teaspoon sifted maple granules (optional), ⅛ cup wheat germ (optional), 2 cups whole wheat pastry flour. Add 3 ounces of milk for every 2 cups of biscuit mix you use in a recipe.

CRUSOE'S SOUTH SEAS SMOOTHY

2 SERVINGS

Drink this only if you wish your timbers to shiver, mate. It's great with whole grain toast sprinkled with cinnamon.

PREP TIME: 5 minutes

- ½ cup skim milk
- 1 cup natural lowfat blueberry yogurt
- ¼ cup natural pineapple-coconut juice
- 1-2 ice cubes

1. Give this stuff a whirl in the blender. Serve in tall glasses. Sprinkle unsweetened coconut on top, if you like.

> "**B**elieve me, my young friend, there is nothing—absolutely nothing—half so much worth doing as simply messing about in boats."
> "The Wind in the Willows"
> by Kenneth Grahame

Sailor's Send-Off

HUNCA MUNCA'S
FRESH-SQUEEZED MUFFINS
◆
NITRATE-FREE
TURKEY SAUSAGES
◆
CRUSOE'S SOUTH
SEAS SMOOTHY
◆

The perfect wake-up if a gaggle of sailors was shipwrecked at your house overnight. Set the table with bandanas as placemats and a favorite toy boat as centerpiece. If you do any real boating, this is an easy meal to prepare in the tiniest galley. You'll find wonderful nitrate-free turkey sausages at natural food stores and some supermarkets.

My Friend, The Germ

Wheat germ may sound like an illness, but it's more like a lifesaver. It's simply the heart of a wheat kernel, and is a great source of vitamin E, the B vitamins, iron and protein. (This is really a breakfast of champions!) Keep it tightly covered and refrigerated, as it contains a vegetable oil that can spoil. Don't be shy about sprinkling some on cereals, bread and cookie batters, soups, shakes and more. If the mere thought of eating something called wheat germ gives you indigestion, try to be brave enough to put a pinch on your finger and lick it off. You'll see right away that it's not even a bit revolting. Tastes sort of like a flat nut, wouldn't you say?

> "*We are plain, quiet folk and have no use for adventures. Nasty, disturbing, uncomfortable things! Make you late for dinner! I can't think what anybody sees in them.*"
> **"The Hobbit" by J.R.R. Tolkien**

SUPER...
CALCIUMPOWERISTICEXTRABERRYDOCIOUS SHAKE

❧ 2 SERVINGS ❧

This is a high-energy meal in a glass, and if you drink it loud enough you'll always sound precocious. Be warned, though, that it's powerful stuff and may put you immediately in the mood for an adventure.

PREP TIME: 5 minutes

> 1 cup lowfat milk
> ½ cup plain lowfat yogurt
> 1 banana, sliced
> 2 tablespoons protein powder*
> 6 strawberries, sliced
> 1 teaspoon wheat germ*
> 1 tablespoon honey or maple syrup
> ¼ cup natural berry juice (such as apple-strawberry)
>   pinch of nutmeg or carob powder

1. Place all but the last ingredient in a blender and mix until smooth. Dust with a sprinkle of nutmeg or carob powder.

*available in natural food stores and supermarket health sections

MONKEY SHINE JUICE

❧ 2 SERVINGS ❧

Here's an easy way to make that everyday glass of orange juice seem special.

PREP TIME: 2 minutes

> 1 cup orange juice
> 1 banana, sliced

1. Place ingredients in a blender and mix until smooth and bubbly.

BUNCHES

*W*hat shall we have for lunch?" he said to the bird.
The bird thought and thought. Finally she said:
Since you're such a beautiful house and since I love you
so much, I should like to fly out and catch some mosquitoes
so that we can have a bit of mosquito pie!"

"Fairy Tales" by e. e. cummings

It's twelve o'clock and all's well—except, of course, that tummies
everywhere are tickling for attention. While mosquito pie
may be a welcome sight on certain tables, we shall hold out
for more civilized and nourishing morsels. After all,
we have half a mind to pack off to the Nile today, if a camel or
two can be located. (Dessert in the desert, anyone?)
After that, there are the usual planets to protect and princes
to rescue and half a zillion stars whose headlights need dusting.
And we haven't once checked the fairy trap we set
at the edge of the forest. We did not forget, however,
to hug the great, kindly evergreen in the woods.
Explorers, poets and princesses—not to mention their Papas
and Mamas—simply cannot put in an extraordinary day
without proper nutrients. Here, to save the day, are
bunches of healthy lunches fit for a kingdom.
If it's a beautiful day, we'll spread a picnic in the shade of
the Great Pyramids. We'll not fail to notice how much
finer everything tastes alfresco (in the open air).
If we're trapped inside by those rascally pirates, Captain Rain or
Captain Snow, we'll get the best of them by making our little
table shine somehow—with a bright, friendly cloth or cupful of
flowers. Afterwards, shall we play a funny record and dance?

OF LUNCHES

MARY'S PEANUT BUTTER & BLUEBERRY MUFFINS

～ 12 MUFFINS ～

This is really the peanut butter and jelly sandwich in disguise, with a handful of fresh fruit added for good measure. It has been known, on occasion, to follow children who have been little lambs to school.

PREP TIME: 15 minutes
BAKING TIME: 20 minutes

    2 **cups whole wheat pastry flour**
 1½ **tablespoons non-aluminum baking powder***
  ½ **cup natural peanut butter**
    2 **eggs**
    4 **tablespoons honey or maple syrup**
  ¾ **cup lowfat milk or soy milk**
  ½ **cup fresh or frozen blueberries**
    1 **jar natural blueberry jam**
      nutmeg

1. Preheat oven to 375°. Coat muffin tins with vegetable oil.
2. In a medium-size mixing bowl, combine flour and baking powder.
3. In a large mixing bowl, combine peanut butter, egg, honey and milk. Add flour mixture. Stir until mixed (batter will be stiff). Fold in blueberries.
4. Fill tins ¾ full with batter. Put a teaspoon or so of jam on top and swirl through batter with a toothpick. Sprinkle top with nutmeg.
5. Bake at 375° for about 20 minutes or until golden brown. Please note that these are heavenly when served warm with a pat of butter or soy margarine.

*available in natural food and gourmet stores

BEAN BAGS

～ 4 SERVINGS ～

These bean and cheese turnovers mix up in a wink with whole grain biscuit mix found in natural food stores. You can also find jars of cooked pinto beans there, or make them yourself. The turnovers are particularly portable, perfect for a packed lunch, and once you taste them, you may want to create other fillings, like apple-tofu or goodness-knows-what.

PREP TIME: 25 minutes
BAKING TIME: 25 minutes

> 2 **cups whole grain biscuit mix**
> 2 **cups cooked pinto beans**
> ¼ **cup natural pickle relish**
> ½ **cup grated Cheddar cheese**
> 2 **tablespoons finely chopped onion**
> 2 **tablespoons natural catsup**
> 1 **tablespoon soy sauce or tamari**
> 1 **egg**
> 3 **tablespoons sesame seeds (optional)**

1. Preheat the oven to 375°.
2. Prepare biscuit mix according to package directions. Roll out dough to about a quarter-inch thickness on a lightly floured surface and cut out 4 circles about 5 inches in diameter (you can measure it with your little ruler). If necessary, re-roll the dough to make the fourth circle.
3. In a medium-size bowl, combine beans, relish, cheese, onion, catsup and tamari. Place about 3 tablespoons of the filling in the center of each dough circle. Fold the dough over to form a half-circle. Press the edges together with a fork to seal.
4. In a small bowl, beat the egg with 1 tablespoon of water. Brush the top of each turnover with the egg mixture and sprinkle generously with sesame seeds.
5. Place on a cookie sheet lined with foil and bake for 25 minutes, until the crust is golden brown.

Serving Suggestion: These are nice with a teaspoon of plain yogurt or sour cream and some salsa on top, if you like hot stuff. A slice of avocado is highly recommended, as well.

Old Lady In A Shoe Box Lunch

BEAN BAGS
◆
SHINY APPLE SLICES
◆
NATURAL CHEESE PUFFS
◆
WHOLE GRAIN
ANIMAL CRACKERS
◆
APPLE JUICE IN A BOX
(store bought juice packaged in a cardboard box)
◆

Round up an equal number of friends and shoe boxes. Wrap them (the boxes, not your friends) in Sunday funny papers or wrapping paper, wrapping top and bottom separately so boxes are easy to open and fill. Then add the food and a picture book. Pass out a box lunch when everyone arrives, and have them try to dress up like the character in the box they get. Everybody will rummage through your room and have a ball trying to dress up. Then eat in costume and let someone read each story aloud (a parent is useful for this part).

RUMPELSTILTSKIN'S PILLOWS

❧ 2 SERVINGS ❧

This is actually a quesadilla, a Mexican grilled cheese of sorts, but think of it as spinning (grating) some straw (cheese) into gold (melted cheese). By any name, it's exceptionally tasty. The finished tortillas, all plump with cheese, look a bit like pillows.

PREP TIME: 5 minutes
COOKING TIME: 5 minutes

- 2 **teaspoons olive oil**
- 2 **large whole wheat tortillas***
- 1½ **cups grated Cheddar or Jack cheese**
- 1 **pinch each ground cumin, cayenne pepper, oregano and thyme or 1 teaspoon natural Mexican Blend seasoning***

1. Heat 1 teaspoon of oil in a large skillet over medium heat. When hot, swirl to coat entire pan and place tortilla in it. After about 1 minute, flip.

2. Place half the cheese on half the surface of the tortilla, and sprinkle with seasonings. After about 1 minute, fold over the empty half to close. Place lid on pan and heat for several minutes, until cheese is just melted. Remove from pan.

3. Repeat with second tortilla. Serve immediately, with any of the Terrific Toppings you like stuffed inside. Cut into wedges to make eating easier.

Terrific Toppings: Shredded lettuce, chopped tomato, yogurt, sour cream, salsa, natural catsup, sliced avocado, sprouts, sunflower seeds.

*available in natural food stores

> **"T**he Queen was terrified, and she offered the little man all the wealth of the kingdom if he would let her keep the child. But the little man said, "No, I would rather have some living thing than all the treasures of the world."
>
> **"Rumpelstiltskin" by the Brothers Grimm**

PETER PIPER'S RED & YELLOW PEPPERED PITA PIZZAS

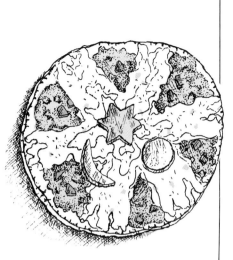

❧ 2 SERVINGS ❧

This is the proverbial pita pizza, but instead of pickled peppers, we'll provide plenty of fiber via the peck of un-pickled peppers we'll pick to place on our pitas. Perhaps we'll cut the peppers in perfectly ridiculous ways, as well. Let's hope Peter approves.

PREP TIME: 10 minutes
BAKING TIME: 5 minutes

  ½ **red and ½ yellow sweet pepper, washed and seeded**
  6 **teaspoons olive oil**
  2 **whole grain pitas**
  2 **tablespoons natural spaghetti sauce or tomato paste**
  ½ **cup grated mozzarella cheese (or other favorite cheese)**
      sprinkle of oregano or Italian Blend Seasonings*

1. Heat 4 teaspoons of oil in a small skillet. With a pair of kitchen scissors, cut stars, sunbursts, moons and other fun shapes out of the sweet peppers. Chop the trimmings and saute them all in the skillet until just a bit soft, about 5 minutes.

2. Spread 1 teaspoon of oil on each pita. Then spread 1 tablespoon of sauce or paste on each pita. Sprinkle with cheese. Decorate with your peppers. Sprinkle with spices.

3. Heat in toaster oven or regular oven on 400° for approximately 5 minutes, or until cheese is bubbly.

*available in natural food stores

CALICO JAM SANDWICHES

❧ 1 SERVING ☙

This is a variation on the old cream-cheese and jelly routine, inspired by a line from Edward Lear's silly, sensational poetry. Try kefir cheese, a rich-tasting yet lowfat alternative to cream cheese, found in natural food stores, that you'll love. The sandwich then gets a crazy quilting of jams, and is cut with a fish-shaped cookie cutter.

PREP TIME: 5 minutes

2 **slices whole grain bread**
2 **tablespoons kefir cheese***
½ **teaspoon each natural grape, blueberry, strawberry and raspberry jam (or any combination of your own favorites)**

1. Spread kefir cheese on a slice of bread. Dot different jams about the cheese in a crazy quilt pattern. Cover with a second slice of bread.
2. Cut with a fish cookie cutter. You could make an eye with a raisin if you care to.

*available in natural food stores

"Calico Jam,
*The little Fish swam,
Over the syllabub sea,
He took off his hat,
To the Sole and the Sprat,
And the Willeby-wat,
But he never came back to me!
He never came back!
He never came back!
He never came back to me!*"
"Calico Pie" by Edward Lear

Wading Pool Picnic

CALICO JAM SANDWICHES
◆
FROZEN SEEDLESS GRAPES
◆
CINNAMON-LEMONADE SLUSH
◆

Cool it by the pool with a silly sandwich cut in a fish shape. Pop the grapes in the freezer early in the morning. And play a cassette tape of "Baby Beluga" by the fabulous children's performer Raffi on your portable tape player.

CUTTING UP

Kids and cookie cutters go together. Those little hunks of tin sleeping in one of your kitchen drawers are the perfect antidote to the boring sandwich. They can make the same old filling seem more enjoyable, as well as making something new and different look admirable enough to try. There are limits, of course. A liver and onion duckie is unlikely to suffer a second bite.

Don't worry about all those odds and ends of bread trimmings, although it's nice to choose cookie cutter sizes that most closely approximate sandwich sizes. But they'll get eaten. You'll munch them. Or the baby will. Or the dog. (Did you know that dogs love whole wheat bread?) And, don't forget there are always hungry birds outside the door.

Here's a few more sandwich ideas that won't wind up on the cutting room floor.

◆ **Peanut Butter & Raspberry Teddies:** Fresh-ground peanut butter on whole grain cinnamon-raisin bread, topped with a handful of fresh raspberries.(Sliced strawberries or blueberries would substitute beautifully.) Cut with a teddy bear cutter. Take them to your own Teddy Bear's Picnic. Don't forget the suncreeen. Bears are delicate and burn easily.

◆ **Puss In Boots:** Put your favorite cheese on whole grain sourdough bread spread with natural mayonnaise, then grate a bit of apple or pear on top. Choose a kitty cutter.

◆ **Hansel & Gretel:** Spread seven-grain bread with cashew butter and unsweetened applesauce, then sprinkle with ginger and cinnamon. Cut with gingerbread boy or girl cutter.

LITTLE MERMAID TUNA MUFFINS

◆ 6 SERVINGS ◆

These petite and portable tuna casseroles neatly balance protein, carbohydrates and fiber. Ideal for using leftover brown rice, which is one of the best of the energy-sustaining complex carbohydrates that are so good for us. They reheat well, especially if topped with a slice of cheese first.

PREP TIME: 20 minutes
BAKING TIME: 40 minutes

- 1 **cup cooked brown rice**
- 4 **tablespoons grated Cheddar cheese**
- 1 **7-oz. can white albacore tuna packed in spring water, drained and flaked**
  dash of pepper
- 5 **tablespoons lowfat yogurt**
- ¼ **apple, cored and finely chopped**
- 1 **tablespoon lemon juice or Honey Lemonade (page 69)**
- 1 **tablespoon chopped parsley**
- 2 **teaspoons tamari or soy sauce**
- 1 **teaspoon grainy mustard**
- 3 **egg whites**

1. Preheat oven to 375°.

2. In a large bowl, combine all ingredients except egg whites and blend.

3. In a medium bowl, beat egg whites with a mixer until stiff peaks form. Fold gently into the tuna mixture.

4. Coat 6 muffin tins well with vegetable oil. Fill with the tuna mixture.

5. Bake 40 minutes or until golden brown on top. Let cool in pan 5 minutes. Run a knife around the edge of each muffin to loosen.

> "**H**uman beings have a soul which lives forever, lives even after the body has turned to earth. It rises through the bright air up to all the shining stars."
> **"The Little Mermaid"**
> **by Hans Christian Andersen**

Bird Watcher's Brunch

FAMILY ROBINSON
CHICKEN SANDWICHES

•

MIXED RAISINS, PEANUTS
& SUNFLOWER SEEDS

•

PINEAPPLE BUBBLE WATER

•

Pack your lunch and binoculars and head for the nearest hill. Sprinkle some of your mixed nuts on the ground about 10 feet away and observe the feathered friends who will soon gather. This is really fun if you have a little book with you to help you identify various birds.

*"**A**nd the nightingale went on singing. It sang about the quiet church-yard where the roses bloom, where the elder flowers scent the air, and where the fresh grass is ever moistened anew by the tears of the mourners."*

"The Nightingale"
by Hans Christian Andersen

FAMILY ROBINSON CHICKEN SALAD

✺ 4 SERVINGS ✺

A shipwreck would seem like paradise with this along, and it makes civilization even more bearable. Don't wait until you have leftover cooked chicken on hand to try it—it's worth the extra effort to make it today. Serve on your favorite whole grain bread or pita half or a bed of crispy lettuce.

PREP TIME: 15 minutes

1½ cups chopped cooked chicken (with skin removed)
1 scallion, finely chopped
⅓ cup chopped, drained pineapple (fresh or canned, in natural juice)
½ cup grated Swiss cheese
3 tablespoons natural mayonnaise
3 tablespoons plain lowfat yogurt
¼ teaspoon curry powder

1. Check to see that your chicken chopping was done well. Then in a medium-size bowl, combine chicken, scallion, cheese and pineapple. Add the yogurt, curry powder and mayonnaise gently.

2. Be prepared for pirates. They love this stuff.

ONCE UPON A WHEAT

One of the healthiest habits to achieve at your house is the regular use of whole grain products, such as bread, rice and cereals. Whole grain bread does not have to taste like the rock of ages. Take the time to seek out the tastiest varieties at natural and gourmet stores and good bakeries. Read ingredients and make sure whole wheat is the first ingredient, not the tenth. Since whole grain products tend to dry out in the refrigerator, it's best to freeze all but enough for a few days, and keep the rest in a bread box. Remember, without preservatives, it has a very short shelf life. Here's a little white lie we concocted at our house to encourage an appreciation of whole grains:

Once upon a time there was a good witch named Wholly, who married Mr. Wheat, the baker. Since witches and bakers do not normally marry, this was very lucky for the world, as you will see. Wholly soon noticed that her hubby was not so very healthy. He was pale and sniffly a lot. She used her witch magic (we call it intuition today) to figure out that Mr. Wheat's troubles started when he had begun milling his wheat flour very fine to make some delicate, sugary creations for the Toothless Fairy. In the process, he had removed the Brave Little Bran and Fabulous Fiber from it, two lovely kinds of fairies that live in every wheat kernel. Scores of vitamins and minerals were sent packing, as well.

Not only were there loads of homeless fairies in the land, but the wheat was now rather empty, nutritionally. It was called White Flour. It looked delicate and tasted like air and became all the rage, but the people who ate lots of it began to look pretty pale themselves, like Mr. Wheat. And they began to put on weight. While it adhered to their hips, they found it did not stick to their ribs—or their walls, either.

You see, many castles and forts were built of bread in those days, and they no longer seemed to hold up when made with White Flour (not to mention the difficulty of keeping a White Castle looking clean). That's when White Flour was first fortified. The baker added bits of vitamins and minerals to it, hoping to make it a better product. But this is where Wholly stepped in and said, "Nonsense, lovey, just go back to the wheat, the whole wheat and nothing but the whole wheat."

Well, Baker Wheat was a wise guy who realized that wives are often so smart and ought to be listened to. And from then on, he made sure that there were fairies galore in the flour that he ground from grain. And lo and behold, the people began to feel better. Their forts were once again strong. Their tummies were once again flat. And the baker gratefully named this wonderful flour after his dear wife.

There is only one sad part to this tale. The laxative makers became very lonely. That, of course, is quite another story!

RUNAWAY BUNNY'S CUSTARD

❧ 4 SERVINGS ❧

*Worth running home for. This is a great new way to love carrots,
cooked tenderly in vegetable stock (available in packages of little
cubes at natural food and gourmet stores), then pureed and topped
with a touch of cheese custard. It's lovely as a side dish with
dozens of dinners, too.*

PREP TIME: 20 minutes
BAKING TIME: 40 minutes

Carrot mixture:
- 1 lb. carrots (5-6), washed, peeled and grated
- ½ cup vegetable stock
- 2 tablespoons olive oil
- 2 tablespoons chopped parsley
- 1 teaspoon tamari or soy sauce
- 1 teaspoon honey (optional)

Custard:
- 2 tablespoons soy margarine
- ¼ cup whole wheat pastry flour
- ½ cup lowfat milk or soymilk
- 3 eggs, beaten
- ¾ cup grated Cheddar cheese
  pinch of nutmeg

1. Preheat oven to 350°.
2. Grate carrots. Place in a medium-size saucepan with stock
and oil. Cover and simmer about 15 minutes, until very tender.
3. While carrots cook, make custard. Melt margarine in a small
saucepan, stir in flour and cook for about 1 minute. Stir in milk
and cook for about 2 minutes. Remove from heat.
4. Stir in eggs and then cheese.
5. Carrots are done! Add parsley,
honey and soy sauce to them,
then blend until fairly smooth
in a blender or processor.
6. Spread carrot mix in
a small, greased casserole
dish. Top with custard
mix, dust with nutmeg
and bake about
40 minutes, or until set.
Serve quite soon.

BERRY BERRY SOUP

4-6 SERVINGS

You must write the real recipe for this soup, creating any combination you like of summer berries and natural berry juice. It's bursting with Vitamin C, which was found to be the cure for beri-beri, a disease that plagued sailors in long ago times. A spectacular summer soup you serve cold.

PREP TIME: 15 minutes
COOKING TIME: 10 minutes
COOLING TIME: 1 hour

2½ **cups water**
1¼ **cups natural berry juice**
  4 **cups any combination blackberries, raspberries, blueberries, strawberries**
 ¼ **cup maple syrup or honey**
 ⅛ **teaspoon ground cloves**
  1 **cinnamon stick**
  1 **lemon**
 ¼ **cup plain lowfat yogurt**

1. In a medium-size saucepan, combine water, berry juice, berries, maple syrup and spices. Bring to a boil over moderate heat. Remove from heat and let cool. Remove cinnamon stick, puree briefly in processor or blender and refrigerate.
2. Top each serving with a dollop of yogurt and a squeeze of lemon juice. Stir to combine before eating.

♦

RED WAGON SOUP

2 SERVINGS

If you want to be a flexible flyer, you ought to eat your soup. This is just the thing for a chilly day and it's fast, so you'll be rolling along in no time. Did you ever write your name on your soup? Or dunk a great whole grain snack in it? Today you shall.

PREP TIME: 5 minutes
COOKING TIME: 5 minutes

1 **small can natural tomato soup**
1 **finely chopped scallion**
1 **tablespoon fresh dill (If possible)**
¼ **cup plain lowfat yogurt at room temperature**

1. In a medium-size saucepan, heat the soup according to package directions. Add scallions while cooking.
2. When hot, pour into bowls and with a small spoon, try and write your name with the yogurt. Add one of these whole grain **Great Garnishes:** Cheese curls, carrot chips, seasoned popcorn, pretzel pieces, corn chips, interesting crackers such as cheese or sesame, or puffed cereal. Top with dill.

> "**G**lorious, stirring sight!" murmured Toad... "The poetry of motion! The real way to travel! The only way to travel! Here today—in next week tomorrow! Villages skipped, towns and cities jumped—always somebody else's horizons! O Bliss! O poop-poop! O my! O my!"
>
> **"The Wind in the Willows" by Kenneth Grahame**

BAMBI'S SALAD BOWL

🎋 2-3 SERVINGS 🎋

Here's a simple salad that children really enjoy. Choose delicate greens for best results.

PREP TIME: 10 minutes

½ **head Boston lettuce, washed and dried**
½ **cup sliced strawberries**
¼ **cup sliced, peeled cucumber**
¼ **cup Honey Lemonade (page 69)**
2 **teaspoons sesame or poppy seeds**

1. Combine lettuce, strawberries and cucumber. Toss with lemonade and sprinkle with seeds.

"Bambi walked under the great oak on the meadow. It sparkled with dew. It smelled of grass and flowers and moist earth, and whispered of a thousand living things."

"Bambi" by Felix Salten

Babes In The Woods Moveable Feast

HANSEL & GRETEL
SANDWICHES

◆

BAMBI'S SALAD

◆

SELFISH GIANT COOKIES

◆

CRANBERRY-APPLE
JUICE IN A BOX

◆

*Tie your lunch up in a big, bright handkerchief and hike to
your favorite woods. Spread the handkerchief under the most
lovable tree you see (even if it's only 10 steps from your door).
Take a few favorite books in your backpack about woodland
animals (Bambi, Velveteen Rabbit, etc.) to look at while you
lunch. Watch for animal footprints, collect leaves or
wildflowers. Try and guess what tune the birds are singing.
Leave a few crumbs of Selfish Giant cookies for them.
Pick up every last scrap of trash to tote back home.*

SNACKS & SIPS

"Time for a little something."
"Winnie-the-Pooh" by A. A. Milne

Afternoon already! Heavens! We have been wondrously busy
today, bursting with good deeds and daring-do.
Even the rocking horse is worn out from riding so often to the
rescue. And yet, a child's work is never done. There's a rash
of measles in the dollhouse to be nursed. (Plenty of bandages
and brownies will put that right.) It's that time of day to be
watchful of witches. And didn't we promise to paint the sunset's
portrait today? (Where is that purple crayon?) Oh, here's a
gracious note from Tarzan inviting us to tea.
Well, one can always find time for a fast safari.
Thank goodness for teatime! Here are several scrumptious
somethings to tide us 'til supper. They're not too sweet.
They're not too hard to make. They're just right. So wherever
you are, gather everyone together for a tray of snacks and sips,
complete with china cups and cheery chitchat.
How grateful we can be not to be living in a time
before the dawn of teatime.

A Little Hint

If you have done something kind and lovely today, remind your Mom or Dad, and suggest that perhaps you deserve a teaspoon or two of pure maple syrup drizzled on your Town Mouse Split. If the direct approach doesn't work, twirl something shiny in front of their eyes for a few minutes, then try again. (By the way, natural food stores sell fruity syrups, such as blueberry and raspberry, that are out of this world. They make a Split that's irresistible.)

TOWN MOUSE'S MINI BANANA SPLIT

2 SERVINGS

Here is a great snack, minus the sweet stuff. A real mouseterpiece. Share it with your friends and you'll be wonderfully popular by this afternoon.

PREP TIME: 5 minutes

1 banana
2 big scoops cottage cheese
   handful of favorite fruit, such as sliced strawberries, blueberries and such
   dash of cinnamon and carob powder
   Assorted Sprinkles

1. Slice banana lengthwise in two pieces, then crosswise. Split between two bowls.

2. Add a scoop of cottage cheese to each bowl, plus a handful of fruit, a dash of cinnamon and carob and your choice of Assorted Sprinkles.

Assorted Sprinkles: Chopped nuts, raisins, sunflower seeds, unsweetened coconut, wheat germ flakes, chopped dried fruit.

"There were sweetmeats and jellies, pastries, delicious cheeses, indeed, the most tempting foods that a Mouse can imagine."
"The Town Mouse and the Country Mouse" by Aesop

Puttin' On The Dog Party

JUMBO'S DELICIOUS DIP

◆

TOFU HOT DOGS WITH ALL THE TRIMMINGS

◆

TOWN MOUSE'S MINI BANANA SPLITS

◆

ONE-TWO PUNCH

◆

Think of this as Animal House for the younger set. Everyone comes with a dog (on a leash) and wearing an apron. You supply the dog brush, shampoo, ribbons and wading pool. Everybody gives their pet a first-rate brushing and bath in the pool with the garden hose, then a neck ribbon of their color choice—while munching on the dip and sipping punch. When the dogs are all clean, each now-perfect pooch gets paraded through a few Dog Show paces: Ask them to roll-over, fetch, sit, etc. Parents will do the judging, but this is nicest when it's declared a tie all-around. Top it all off with the Tofu Hot Dogs from the natural food store— nitrate-free Hot Dogs are nice, too—and Banana Splits for everyone. How about a round of biscuits for the canine crowd? (By the way, it's more fun if you only invite very friendly dogs to this particular party.)

Red Wagon Tea Service

BEST BELOVED
CRACKER BITES

♦

TINKER BELL'S
RASPBERRY BUNS

♦

CINNAMON APPLE
HERB TEA WITH MILK

♦

COLD APPLE JUICE

♦

*Lay a lacy cloth across
your wagon and wheel
this feast across the lawn
to the waiting guests. You
can be certain you will be
cheered.*

BEST BELOVED CRACKER BITES

❧ SEVERAL SERVINGS ❧

This idea has been around since High & Far-off Times. It's really just crackers with nice tasty morsels heaped on top. The way it became popular again in Modern Times is this: Mrs. Mama Kipling used to leave a plate of them for her dear son Rudyard, always with a note lying beside that began, "For my Best Beloved…" Always start with a great whole grain cracker. Experiment with the wide array of tasty varieties at natural foods stores and supermarket health sections. And go to town on the toppings:

♦ Chunky peanut butter with a slice of apple on top.
♦ A slice of Cheddar cheese with a slice of apple on top.
♦ A slice of Brie cheese and a slice of strawberry.
♦ A heap of Roquefort cheese topped with a piece of pear.
♦ Spread a cheese cracker with mustard. Top with Havarti cheese and fresh-ground pepper.
♦ Top a dash of kefir cheese or cream cheese with a dried apple ring.
♦ Spread cracker with a dab of natural mayonnaise. Place slice of hard-boiled egg on top and sprinkle gently with paprika.
♦ Top a heap of Montrachet (that's goat cheese, but you mustn't let that stop you or you're likely to be called a chicken) with a dab of natural orange marmalade.

A Little Hint

When making your Cracker Bites, it's nice to know about the most important rule of food decorating, also referred to as The Forces of Light & Dark. To make a long story short, when you're trying to make food look pretty, top light things with dark things, and dark things with light things. For example: coconut shavings don't do much for cream cheese. And chopped parsley will fail to improve the way spinach looks. It's that simple.

"**B**efore the High and Far-Off Times, O my Best Beloved, came the time of the very Beginning; and that was in the days when the Eldest Magician was getting Things ready. First he got the Earth ready; then he got the Sea ready; and then he told all the Animals they could come out and play."

"Just So Stories" by Rudyard Kipling

PETER & BENJAMIN'S BUNNY CAKE

6-8 SERVINGS

This is a savory, not sweet, cake—but you'll be delighted at how delicious it is, anyway. Worth slipping into Farmer MacGregor's garden to borrow a few carrots for.

PREP TIME: 15 minutes
COOKING TIME: 20-25 minutes

- 2 cups washed, peeled carrots, grated
- 1 cup whole grain biscuit mix
- 7 tablespoons grated Parmesan cheese
- ¼ cup olive or other vegetable oil
- 2 eggs, beaten
- ½ onion, finely chopped
- 2 tablespoons chopped parsley
- 1 teaspoon oregano
- 1 tablespoon tamari or soy sauce

1. Preheat oven to 350°.
2. Place all ingredients in large bowl and stir well.
3. Spread the mixture in a 9-inch square pan greased with vegetable oil and bake for 20 to 25 minutes, until a bit brown.
4. It's tastiest served slightly warm.

A Little Hint

Several tablespoons of grated vegetables, such as carrots or zucchini, are a great addition to packaged whole grain bread, pancake and muffin mixes.

It not only makes a moister batter, but it adds precious vitamins and minerals, as well.

If you have the extra time, saute the vegetables in a bit of vegetable broth or oil, for even more flavor. Try it with this recipe using ¼ cup broth, and see if you don't agree.

True Blue

Did you know that there was a real Peter Rabbit and a real Benjamin Bunny (he was nicknamed Bounce)? They were childhood pets of Beatrix Potter, the artist who created those adventurous little characters in print. They lived right in her very own bedroom in a house in London, and loved nothing better than a warm hearth to sleep on. Peter would lay cuddled up in front of the fireplace on top of an old blue quilt that he seemed particularly fond of. And that is how the fancy coat that caused him such a fright in "The Tale of Peter Rabbit" came to be painted blue by Beatrix Potter.

JUMBO'S DELICIOUS DIP
WITH CRUDITÉ TRUNKS

❧ SEVERAL SERVINGS ❧

Jumbo, once the biggest star in P. T. Barnum's circus, used to whip this up for all his friends at the circus, including that famous little elephant who learned to fly. When you're done eating this, you should have the energy to "believe and soar," just as he did.

PREP TIME: 5 minutes

- ½ **cup natural peanut butter**
- ½ **cup plain lowfat yogurt**
- 1 **tablespoon pure maple syrup or honey**
  celery stalks

1. Please have peanut butter at room temperature, then blend all ingredients together and serve with Crudité Trunks.

Crudité Trunks: Take stalks of celery and try to think of them as elephant noses. Why would a grey elephant have a green trunk, you ask? Remember the old Elephant in "The Story of Babar" who turned green after eating a certain kind of mushroom? (Well, have you a better explanation?)

Other great dippers for this dip are raw carrot curls, whole grain pretzel sticks, rippled natural potato chips and pieces of fruit, especially banana chunks.

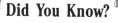

Did You Know?

Crudité is a French word that is used to refer to uncooked vegetables. Knowing this may make all the difference for you should you find yourself on a quiz show one day.

"**H**ow do you know I am lying?"
"Lies, my boy, are known in a moment. There are two kinds of lies, lies with short legs and lies with long noses. Yours, just now, happen to have long noses."
"Pinocchio"
by Carlo Collodi

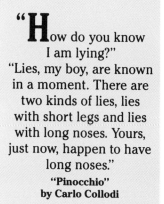

A LITTLE HINT

Top each moon with sliced fresh fruit and a teaspoon of natural jam. Here's some happy combinations: fresh nectarines or peaches with blueberry or raspberry jam, fresh raspberries with orange marmalade, and fresh strawberries with natural applesauce or apple butter.

AMY'S LITTLE CHEESE MOONS

MAKES OVER 2 DOZEN

These thin cheese biscuits are quickly mixed, shaped by cookie cutter into half-moons and baked in just 10 minutes. They're delicately crunchy and delicious, especially when topped with sliced fresh fruit and a teaspoon of your favorite natural jam. They're named in honor of Amy March, the youngest heroine of Louisa May Alcott's "Little Women."

PREP TIME: 20 minutes
BAKING TIME: 10 minutes

- 1¾ cups grated cheddar cheese
- 1 cup whole wheat pastry flour
- 5 tablespoons soy margarine
  cinnamon

1. Preheat oven to 400°. Coat with vegetable oil and lightly dust with flour a cookie sheet.
2. Grate cheese in a food processor, then remove and measure. Return cheese to processor and add flour and margarine, cutting it into several chunks. Process with the metal blade for about 30 seconds, until a fairly smooth dough is formed.
3. Dust your hands with flour to keep things from getting too sticky. Take tablespoons of dough and form into a patty about ⅛-inch thick (if you make them thicker, they won't taste quite as nice). Cut with a moon cutter and place on the cookie sheet. Create many moons this way, using all the dough.
5. Dust each moon with cinnamon and bake for about 10 minutes. Let cool on sheet before removing.

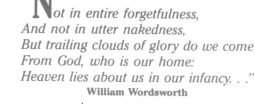

Not in entire forgetfulness,
And not in utter nakedness,
But trailing clouds of glory do we come
From God, who is our home:
Heaven lies about us in our infancy. . ."
William Wordsworth

~ NURSERY SNACKS ~

Heaven really does seem to shine on a home with a baby in it. Naturally, the "little creature formed of joy and mirth" that William Blake wrote of deserves special attention when it comes time for his or her first cuisine.

Here's a diaper-bag worth of hints and ideas:

◆ **SOLID SUCCESS:** Many experts today suggest waiting 6 months to start foods, especially if there's any history of allergies in the family. Babies have opinions of their own, however. They hint by growing teeth and grabbing food out of people's hands.

◆ **THE NEXT MOOOVE:** Some pediatricians advise withholding cow's milk even longer. Plain yogurt is an ideal first dairy food. Its beneficial bacteria help baby's stomach do the digesting. Some babies will take yogurt plain, but others will need a tiny bit of maple syrup swirled in to convince them. At one year, you can sweeten it deliciously with orange juice concentrate (acidity can be a problem until then).

◆ **GOODBYE, MY HONEY:** Avoid honey as a sweetener for infants under one year. They can contract a form of food poisoning called infant botulism from it. After a year, their digestive tracts are developed enough to handle it. Pureed fruits, such as applesauce, fruit juices, a touch of unsweetened jam, and maple syrup or granules are all nice alternatives. But it's best to keep all sweeteners to a minimum.

◆ **THE DAILY GRIND:** Baby food grinders mash fruit and cooked vegetables and cereals into a baby-perfect puree quick as a wink. They're very inexpensive and wonderfully easy to clean—quite preferable to processors when making small quantities. Some ideal first pureed foods, according to nutrition experts: bananas, pears, papayas, apples, cooked yellow vegetables, and cereals made of rice, barley or oats.

◆ **RED ALERT:** It's wise to introduce new foods one at a time, so that you'll be able to easily spot a food that's produced an allergic reaction.

◆ **SECOND STRING:** Potatoes and pureed green vegetables are nice secondary introductions. After nine months of age, some peeled, chopped raw fruits and raw vegetables are welcomed, as are wheat bread (buttered whole grain toast is always a hit) and cheese. Fresh fruit salad, either raw or baked in the oven until soft, is a delicious treat.

◆ **TOOTH OR CONSEQUENCES:** For teething pain, try offering a frozen banana on a stick. Look in natural food stores for whole grain baby biscuits and cereals (such as fruit flavored rings) that make ideal finger foods.

GOLDEN GLOVES

Here's a pretty puree, named after where much of it winds up: Chop 1 cup acorn or butternut squash and ½ cup peeled red apple (not a tart variety). Place in a buttered dish and drizzle with ⅓ cup yogurt or breast or soy milk (depending on baby's age). Bake, covered, for 40 minutes at 325°. Puree in baby food grinder or blender. You can make this in quantity and freeze in ice cube trays. After it's frozen, transfer the cubes to small bags to thaw and warm as needed.

PEACHY RICE CAPADES

. . . Is pure pleasure. Puree 1 cup peeled, ripe peaches or nectarines. Mix with 2 cups cooked brown rice and several table-spoons apple juice in a buttered baking dish and bake at 350° for 15 to 20 minutes. When finished, swirl in ¼ cup plain yogurt and sweeten with a touch more apple juice, if needed. You can puree the final product in your baby grinder for a smoother texture.

MOM'S MAPLY CARROTS

. . . Are a must: Grate 5 to 6 carrots and cook, covered, in ⅔ cup vegetable broth until tender, about 10 minutes. Transfer to blender or processor, add a teaspoon or two of pure maple syrup and puree until smooth. Thin with a bit of yogurt or add to cottage cheese, if you like.

> "*I will surely come,*" *said Mowgli; "and when I come it will be to lay out Shere Khan's hide upon the Council Rock. Do not forget me! Tell them in the Jungle never to forget me!*"
> *The dawn was beginning to break when Mowgli went down the hillside alone, to meet those mysterious things that are called men.*"
>
> **"The Jungle Book"**
> **by Rudyard Kipling**

Tricycle Rally Starters

PETER & BENJAMIN'S
BUNNY CAKE

◆

MOWGLI'S TIGER MILK

◆

Invite a few friends for a cycling obstacle course on your lawn. Set up big empty boxes, old tires, croquet markers, etc. Serve the above snacks at a little table set up on the starting line. Tell everyone these foods are the snacks of champions. After it's all had time to settle in your tummies and call forth reserves of strength and power you only dared dream of, it's time for the race. Winner gets a Tricycle Olympics Certificate you've crayoned yourself, along with a plate of Baloo's Mint Brownies (page 85). Who knows? Perhaps she'd even share them with a bunch of good-humored runners-up.

MOWGLI'S TIGER MILK

2 SERVINGS

It is just this drink that gave the brave Mowgli, of Rudyard Kipling's "Jungle Book," the strength to overcome the villainous tiger, Shere Khan. Mowgli's descendents passed the recipe on to Gayelord Hauser. A pioneer of the health movement who lived to a vibrant 89, Mr. Hauser once said, "Whatever your present age, you are young." This milk put hair on Mowgli's chest and will no doubt do the same for you.

PREP TIME: 5 minutes

> 1 cup whole milk
> 1 cup orange juice
> 2 teaspoons skim milk powder
> 1 teaspoon molasses
> 1 teaspoon Brewer's yeast or wheat germ*

1. Blend in a blender until smooth and serve chilled.
2. Try to resist the urge to bend steel with your bare hands.

*available in natural food stores and supermarket health sections

CINNAMON LEMONADE SLUSH

2 SERVINGS

Different and delightful, and just the thing for a deliriously hot day. But here's a funny secret: It's just as good served warm on a wickedly cold day.

PREP TIME: 2 minutes
COOKING TIME: 5 minutes
COOLING TIME: 20 minutes

> 2 cups Honey Lemonade (page 69)
> 1 cinnamon herb tea bag

1. In a small saucepan, add herb tea bag to lemonade and gently heat for about 5 minutes. Remove tea bag and chill.
2. Serve over crushed ice.

CURIOUS GEORGE SLUSH

~1 SERVING~

A tropical vacation. If you want to make it really curious, freeze the banana first. Happy and sad days alike seem better after a slug of this stuff.

PREP TIME: A minute

    1 **cup natural pineapple-coconut juice**
    1 **banana, sliced**
4-6 **ice cubes**

1. Give the ingredients a ride in the blender. When they look smooth, pour and drink.

PINEAPPLE BUBBLE WATER

~2 SERVINGS~

Fizzy and refreshing and ridiculously easy.

PREP TIME: A minute

1 **cup natural pineapple juice**
1 **cup sparkling water**

1. Mix and serve over ice. Dunk a fresh cherry or slice of apple in it.

JACK FROST CHASER

~2 SERVINGS~

Did you know that Johnny Appleseed and Jack Frost were best friends? It was usually the dead of winter when Jack would blow into town and the two liked to sit and talk about their wonderful work over a cup of this delicious hot beverage. Problem was, Johnny could never get Jack to be on his way and…Anyway, do try it yourself.

PREP TIME: 5 minutes
COOKING TIME: 10 minutes

4 **apple herbal tea bags**
1 **tablespoon honey**
1 **cup apple juice**
1 **cup pineapple juice**
2 **teaspoons Honey Lemonade (page 69)**

1. Bring two cups of water to a boil and add tea bags. Turn heat off and let steep for 5 minutes.
2. Remove tea bags and stir in honey, apple and pineapple juices and lemonade. Heat gently but do not boil.
3. Serve in a cup with cinnamon stick.

A Little Hint

Sparkling waters come with various essences or flavorings these days: Orange, lemon, lime, cherry, etc. You can make outstanding natural sodas by pairing these with your favorite natural juices. Actually, that's very healthy, since it reduces the sugar content of the juice (even if it's natural sugar, most of us could do with cutting down a bit). Try orange juice mixed with cherry water or grape juice mixed with orange water. To make a great favorite called **Berry Bubble Water,** just mix any natural strawberry juice with your favorite sparkling water. Plop a fat, ripe strawberry in it, too.

WHAT'S
IN A
NAME?

It is said that the Oz in
L. Frank Baum's classic
"Wizard of Oz" acquired
its name in a most curious
manner. Mr. Baum kept a
three-drawer filing
cabinet in his office. The
third file was marked
with a label "O-Z" to
indicate its alphabetical
contents, and the writer's
glance just happened to
fall there as he searched
for the perfect name for
his Emerald City.

ONE-TWO PUNCH

15 or SO SERVINGS

*For kids who go for a bit of bubbly, this provides quite a kick.
Great for crowd control.*

PREP TIME: 2 minutes

> 1 qt. chilled sparkling apple juice
> 2 qts. chilled natural cherry cider*

1. Mix and gulp. In smaller quantities, it's ridiculously good
served over crushed ice, but that can get messy for a crowd.
Some people, of course, prefer a crowd that's messy. Seldom
does this group include parents, however.

*available in natural food stores and supermarket health sections

PENGUIN PUNCH

2 SERVINGS

What's brown and white and cool all over?

PREP TIME: 2 minutes

> 2 scoops carob ice cream
> 1 cup cold soymilk or lowfat milk
> 1 cup cold natural tangerine or orange soda

1. Divide the milk and soda between two tall glasses.
Mix 'em up and add a scoop of ice cream to each.

OVER THE RAINBOW MILK

2 SERVINGS

*The music of childhood is sometimes curious. You really must
be a child to like these Technicolored glasses of milk, made
simply with milk and natural fruit juice. But as sure as the
Yellow Brick Road ends at Oz, if you're a child, you'll like them.
Choose the hue of your choice. Imagine a birthday party with a
different one set at each place!*

PREP TIME: About a minute

> 1 cup lowfat milk
> ½ cup pure fruit juice (such as grape, cherry, apricot,
> pineapple, etc.)

1. Combine, stir and sip.
2. You're not off to see the wizard—you are the wizard!

THE SUPPER

Today, we were as happy as the sky was blue. And now sailors, snowman makers, ballerinas and bareback riders come marching home before Madam Sunshine takes her leave. It will take a wonderful supper indeed to bring worn-out little ones enough energy to finish those last duties left undone.

There's a four-star mess in the nursery to tidy. The lawn is blanketed with sailboats, rubber balls, tin soldiers and tea service for four. (Don't forget Dolly and Bunny taking some fresh air over by the tulip bed.) Miss Kitty is calling for her dinner dish. And Papa promised to accompany you outside tonight with a lighted candle so you could invite the evening wind to blow it out.

The Supper Club convenes only when all ten fingers have been scrubbed clean and inspected. First, why not surprise everyone by gathering a few leaves and flowers in a pretty basket to grace your happy table? The poet Samuel Taylor Coleridge wrote, "Earth, with her thousand voices, praises God." Shall we join that chorus and thank the Eldest Magician for the bounty upon our table?

CLUB

"*I*f I could find a higher tree
Farther and farther I should see,
To where the grown up river slips
Into the sea among the ships,

To where the roads on either hand
Lead onward into fairy land,
Where all the children dine at five
And all the playthings come alive."

"A Child's Garden of Verses"
by Robert Louis Stevenson

A Little Hint

Removing the skin on chicken is one good way to reduce fat in your diet, although skin is said to hold in juices during cooking. Soaking chicken in liquid, or marinade, before cooking is a good way to make up for this, and be sure of a moist, tender meal. For simple broiled chicken to which you are not adding any coating, you can remove the skin after cooking.

AESOP'S FABLED CHICKEN

ꞋꞋꞋꞋ 4 SERVINGS ꞋꞋꞋꞋ

A treasured recipe, passed down through countless generations of the family Aesop. After bathing in a peanut butter and peach juice marinade, the chicken is rolled in fairy dust (crushed cornflakes and seasonings) before baking. Sounds a bit unusual, but it eats like ambrosia.

PREP TIME: 15 minutes
MARINATING TIME: 1 hour
BAKING TIME: 45 minutes

- 4 **large pieces chicken with skin removed (boned breasts are especially nice)**
- 2 **tablespoons natural peanut butter (at room temperature)**
- 2 **tablespoons melted soy margarine**
- 1 **cup natural peach or apricot juice**
- 2 **cups whole grain cornflakes, crushed**
- ½ **teaspoon powdered ginger**
  pinch of pepper

1. In a shallow pan or bowl, mix peanut butter, margarine and juice. Place chicken pieces in pan and refrigerate for at least one hour, turning once.
2. Preheat oven to 350°.
3. Mix the cornflakes, ginger and pepper in a shallow bowl, or on waxed paper. Take each piece of chicken from the juice and roll it in the cornflakes, coating both sides well.
4. Place chicken on a rack in a baking pan that you've covered with foil. Drizzle a tablespoon of the leftover juice on each piece.
5. Bake for 45 minutes, pouring a bit more juice on each piece once or twice during the baking process.

> **"D**o not count your chickens before they are hatched!"
> **"The Milkmaid & Her Pail" by Aesop**

THE TALE OF AESOP

There are nearly as many tales about who Aesop actually was as there are fables attributed to him. Perhaps the most popular claims that he was a black Ethiopian (that's what Aesop means) who lived as a slave some five hundred years before the birth of Christ. He supposedly won his freedom and eventually became an ambassador of sorts to a rich king named Croesus, visiting the king's various regions where he often told stories to make a certain point. He is said to have put the stories in the form of animal fables, each with an important message, in order to avoid offending his human audience. Another idea is that the many fables attributed to Aesop were really told by a whole group of wise slaves of that time period. Part of the legend even holds that Aesop was eventually hurled off a high cliff for offending the king by becoming a bit too wise for his own good. Not a very happy ending for Aesop, was it?

CURIOUSER & CURIOUSER CASSEROLE

❧ 10-12 SERVINGS ❧

This dish is a tasty bit of Jabberwocky. Think of it as a chili-pasta-spaghetti sauce-corn-cheese casserole, of sorts. The ingredient list looks long, but make it in a wok, and you'll discover it's a one-dish wonder that will quickly quiet a crowd who've come down with the hungries.

PREP TIME: 15 minutes
COOKING TIME: 35-40 minutes

- 4 **cups natural spaghetti sauce**
- 2 **15-oz. cans natural vegetarian chili (with or without beans)**
- 1 **lb. cooked whole grain elbow or spiral noodles, drained**
- 1 **package frozen corn kernels, thawed but uncooked**
- 1 **onion, finely chopped**
- 2 **bell peppers, seeded and finely chopped**
- ½ **cup chopped fresh cilantro (parsley will also do)**
- 2 **cups grated Cheddar cheese**
- 2-3 **scallions, chopped finely (optional)**
- 1 **large bag natural corn tortilla chips**

1. Place wok over moderately high heat. Add pasta sauce and chili, stirring to combine. Add corn and mix well.
2. Add onion, peppers and cilantro and stir. Reduce heat to moderately low and simmer for 15 minutes, stirring often.
3. Add noodles and cook for 10 to 15 minutes, until the sauce has reduced a bit.
4. Remove from heat. Sprinkle cheese evenly over the surface. Cover for 10 minutes, until cheese melts. Garnish with chopped scallions. (You can take it to the table right in the wok, and lift the lid at the last minute.)
5. To serve, place some of the corn chips on each plate and top with Casserole.

"**C**uriouser and curiouser!" cried Alice (she was so much surprised, that for the moment she quite forgot how to speak good English)."

"Alice's Adventures in Wonderland" by Lewis Carroll

MUCHNESS TOMATO BISCUITS

⇜ 18 2-INCH BISCUITS ⇝

Quick, quick biscuits made with packaged whole grain biscuit mix and vegetable juice. Parents will like them even more with a few tablespoons of salsa added to the dough or served on top after cooking. In either case, they're great with a bowl of chili, soup or stew. While fresh herbs add much, much flavor, dried herbs will work also, though you can reduce the quantity.

PREP TIME: 15 minutes
BAKING TIME: 10 minutes

- **2 cups whole grain biscuit mix**
- **1 cup mixed vegetable juice (like V-8)**
- **¼ cup safflower oil or soy margarine, melted**
- **2 tablespoons chopped fresh basil, parsley, cilantro or oregano**

1. Preheat the oven to 375°.

2. In a large bowl, combine all ingredients. Roll out the dough on a lightly floured surface to ¼-inch thickness and cut into 2-inch rounds with an upside-down glass or a biscuit cutter, if you have one.

3. Transfer biscuits to a baking sheet lightly greased with vegetable oil, sprinkle fresh herbs on top and bake for 10 minutes, just until the edges begin to brown.

A Little Hint

You can experiment with many other kinds of Muchness Biscuits by simply using fruit juice in place of the vegetable juice. For **Muchness Berry Biscuits,** try 1 cup of your favorite berry juice, plus ½ cup of raisins. Before baking, top each with a bit of maple syrup. How about Apple Biscuits, Grape Biscuits, Pineapple Biscuits—let there be a method in your muchness!

"They drew all manner of things— everything that begins with an M . . . such as mousetraps, and the moon, and memory, and muchness—you know how you say things are 'much of a muchness.'"

"Alice's Adventures in Wonderland" by Lewis Carroll

Delicious Double Feature

FROG PRINCE
TORTILLA PIE

♦

ONE-TWO PUNCH

♦

MARY POPPINS' AMAZING
PEACHY PIE

♦

Have friends over for a little Silver Screen Festival and Feast. Round-up or rent a few all-time favorites (like Mary Poppins, The Muppets or a few Fairy Tale Theatres). Put some little tables up in front of your telly. Decorate tabletops with hand-colored cut-outs of the movie characters from coloring books (back with cardboard to stand up). Any appropriate stuffed animals (like a Muppet Baby) you have on hand would do nicely, too. All the food can be made ahead, so there's no last-minute rushing around. Just sit back and laugh.

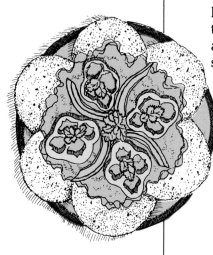

FROG PRINCE TORTILLA PIE

⇝ 6 SERVINGS ⇜

Prepared foods are often pooh-poohed by health purists, but if they're of high quality, they can be quickly transformed into something quite handsome. Corn tortillas make an appealing, petal-shaped crust in the wink of an eye.

PREP TIME: 20 minutes
BAKING TIME: 35 minutes

- 6 **corn tortillas**
- 2 **cups grated Jack cheese**
- 1 **8-oz. can natural vegetarian chili with beans**
- 1 **small can prepared jalapeno or onion dip***
- 1 **teaspoon Mexican Blend seasonings* or pinch of ground cumin, cayenne, oregano and thyme**
- 2 **eggs**
- 1½ **cups soymilk**

1. Preheat oven to 325°.
2. Line a 9-inch pie pan with the tortillas, overlapping them, and extending them about half an inch over the edge of the pan. Sprinkle half your cheese over the tortillas.
3. In a medium-size bowl, mix the chili, bean dip and seasonings and spread evenly on top of the cheese.
4. In a small bowl, beat eggs with milk and pour over chili mixture. Sprinkle with remaining cheese.
5. Bake for about 35 minutes, until the top is just beginning to firm—it will firm more as it cools.

Decorating Ideas: This looks lively with 4 red pepper or tomato rings on top and several avocado slices intertwined among them. Sprigs of fresh cilantro are a wonderful sight and scent here, too.

*Available in natural foods stores

"**I**n that moment
he was no longer
a cold, fat, goggle-eyed frog,
but a young Prince
with handsome friendly eyes."

"The Frog Prince"
by the Brothers Grimm

LOST BOYS' TOFU KEBABS

4-6 SERVINGS

Named in honor of Peter Pan's compatriots, the children who fell out of their carriages when their nursemaids weren't looking and wound up in Neverland. This is a different kind of kebab, coated with a luscious apple barbecue sauce. Just wait 'til you taste it hot off the grill this summer!

PREP TIME: 15 minutes
COOKING TIME: 10-15 minutes

- ½ **cup natural barbecue sauce**
- 1 **tablespoon grainy mustard**
- ½ **cup natural apple juice**
- 1 **cake tofu, cut into small cubes (about the size of a cherry tomato)**
- ½ **pint cherry tomatoes**
- 10 **small mushrooms, stalks removed**
- 1 **apple, unpeeled, cut into small chunks chunks of favorite summer vegetables, such as baby eggplant or squash**

1. Combine barbecue sauce, mustard and juice in a bowl. Add tofu cubes and mix well, then place in the refrigerator for an hour.

2. On metal skewers, alternate tofu chunks with other ingredients. Coat everything with the barbecue mixture, using a small brush. Grill over hot coals for about 5 minutes on each side, brushing with more marinade when you turn. Remember that metal skewers will get hot, so don't lift with your bare fingers. To serve, remove from skewers and serve over brown or wild rice.

A Little Hint

On a rainy or frozen day, you can still make these kebabs. Just place them on a broiler pan covered with foil and broil for 5 minutes on each side, turning and brushing with more marinade. Be sure to set the oven rack about 5 inches from the heating element for broiling, so that the food to be cooked is about 3 inches from the heating element.

Lost Boys' Buffet

LOST BOYS' TOFU KEBABS ◆ GRAPE BUBBLE WATER
HIAWATHA'S CUSTARDY CORN BREAD ◆ LIONS & TIGERS & BEARS, OH MY!

*All is not lost, even though you're entertaining ten or so wild little Indians.
What could be more fun than kebabs, corn bread and cupcakes?
Combine grape juice and sparkling water (half and half) to make the bubble
water. You could have beads (from a craft store) and feathers (gathered from
the ground and spray painted bright colors) for table decorations. You could
play Pin the Hook on the Pirate (make a hook from silver foil and crayon a
Captain Hook if you can't find a picture). If it's summer and you've got a
pool, everyone must Walk The Plank (diving board)! Don't forget to play the
soundtrack from the Disney movie "Peter Pan."*

BIRD IN THE FOREST

4 SERVINGS

This was inspired by a traditional Chinese dish, so serve it to your most honorable guests. Sliced Honey-Lemonade Chicken (the bird) sits in a clearing surrounded by a ring (forest) of steamed broccoli. Bursting with nutrients and so beautiful!

PREP TIME: 20 minutes
COOKING TIME: 20 minutes

- **2 cups sliced Honey Lemonade Chicken**
- **3 cups fresh broccoli spears**
- **½ cup Honey Lemonade Butter Sauce**

1. Prepare Honey Lemonade Chicken: Marinate 4 large chicken breasts (with skin removed) in 2 cups of Honey Lemonade (see page 69) for at least one hour in the refrigerator. Save juice. Broil chicken on a foil-covered pan in the oven for 8 to 10 minutes on each side, basting each side with a teaspoon of honey or maple syrup.

2. Put a large saucepan of water on to boil. Cut broccoli florets (that's a single clump) into pieces about 2 inches long. Discard the stalks. Place broccoli in boiling water for 3 to 4 minutes, then drain and place right away in a pan of cold water to stop them from cooking. Drain after 2 to 3 minutes.

3. Prepare Honey Lemonade Butter Sauce: In broccoli pan, combine 4 tablespoons of soy margarine with ½ cup Honey Lemonade. Stir and heat gently until butter is melted. Add broccoli back to pan and toss until coated.

4. To serve, cut chicken into strips about 2″ long and mound in a circle around center of plate. Lay broccoli florets in a ring around the chicken, standing them up to resemble trees. You can put one "tree" in the center of the chicken, if you like.

A Nutty Idea

Here's a quick sauce you can toss cooked brown rice in that goes nicely with Bird In The Forest. For each 2 cups of rice, combine 1 tablespoon of peanut butter, 1 tablespoon of honey, 2 tablespoons of soy sauce (shoyu is nice here), ½ teaspoon of ground ginger, 2 tablespoons of mineral (or plain) water and 2 tablespoons of Honey Lemonade. If you like, add a chopped scallion or two, too. Toss to coat your cooked rice.

HIAWATHA'S CUSTARDY CORN BREAD

❧ 6-8 SERVINGS ❧

The fabulously milky, sweet flavor of fresh corn kernels and the custard-like texture of this cornbread combine to make a heavenly taste. When the corn is as high as an elephant's eye in the fields, you'll know it's time to forage for this recipe.

PREP TIME: 15 minutes
BAKING TIME: 35-40 minutes

> "**A**t the door on
> summer evenings
> Sat the little Hiawatha;
> Heard the whispering
> of the pine trees,
> Heard the lapping
> of the waters,
> Sounds of music,
> words of wonder;
> "Minne-wawa!"
> said the pine trees,
> "Mudway-aushka!"
> said the water."
>
> **"The Song of Hiawatha"
> by Henry Wadsworth
> Longfellow**

2 cups whole grain corn muffin mix
  kernels from two ears of corn (about 1½ cups)
2 cups soy milk
2 eggs, beaten
⅓ cup honey or pure maple syrup
¼ cup vegetable oil
  dash of salt and pepper

1. Preheat oven to 350°.
2. In a large bowl, mix all ingredients with a whisk. Spread in an 8-inch square pan greased with vegetable oil or soy margarine. (A glass pan is nice if you'd like to serve it in the pan, since it will look sensational.) Bake until top is golden and a bit crusty, but interior is still custardy, about 35 minutes.

STEADFAST TIN SOLDIER FILETS

❧ 6 SERVINGS ❧

Created in memory of Hans Christian Andersen's proud yet humble toy soldier with only one leg who remained at attention even as he lay in the belly of a fish. And whose love for the little paper ballerina remained steadfast to the end.

PREP TIME: 10 minutes
BAKING TIME: 15 minutes

- **2 pounds boned, skinned flounder filets (or other favorite fish filets)**
- **½ cup Honey Lemonade**
- **1½ cups crushed whole grain crackers**
- **1 teaspoon paprika**
- **2 tablespoons chopped fresh parsley**
- **1 tablespoon chopped fresh chives**

1. Preheat oven to 350°.
2. Pat fish filets with paper towels to dry them. Place the lemonade in a bowl and combine the next 2 ingredients in a second bowl. Dip the filets in the lemonade and then in the crumb mixture, coating completely.
3. Place the filets on a rack to settle while you're preparing the rest.
4. With scissors, cut tin foil in the outline of a fish big enough to hold one filet. (You needn't be too perfect about all this, and if it seems too tough, simply line a baking sheet with foil.) Place filets on the foil, place foil on a baking sheet and sprinkle fish with the fresh herbs.
5. Bake for 15 minutes. Leave filets on individual fish foils when serving on plates.

"The tin soldier melted down into a lump, and when the servant took the ashes out next day, she found him there in the shape of a little tin heart."

"The Steadfast Tin Soldier"
by Hans Christian Andersen

68

HONEY LEMONADE:
A COOK'S MAIN SQUEEZE

You'll find wonderful bottled lemonade sweetened with honey or fruit juice in natural food stores and supermarket health sections, or you can make your own quite easily:

For each cup of water, you add 1½ tablespoons each fresh lemon juice and honey. Boil water and honey for 2 minutes. Remove from heat and add lemon juice. Store in a jar in the refrigerator.

It's a great item to keep on hand. You can use it in every kind of recipe in place of plain lemon juice, which to a child often tastes too tart. You can sprinkle it over fresh fruit to keep the fruit from darkening. You can splash it on your salad or broiled fish. You can marinate chicken and fish in it before cooking. You can even just drink it.

THUMBELINA BURGERS

〜 4-5 SERVINGS 〜

These little tofu-beef meatballs are served between whole wheat crackers with a marvelous pineapple-mustard sauce. You can make regular-size burgers for the adults if they don't care to be quite so silly. By the way, the tofu cuts the cholesterol content of the beef by a third, and the fat content by one-fourth.

PREP TIME: 15 minutes
COOKING TIME: 10 minutes

- 1 lb. lean ground beef
- 8 oz. soft tofu
- 1 cup chopped, drained pineapple (fresh or canned, packed in natural juice)
- 2 tablespoons grainy mustard
- 1 package favorite round whole grain crackers (or cut tiny circles out of whole grain bread)

1. In large bowl, mash the tofu carefully. Add the ground beef and mix well. Roll into meatball-size burgers, flattening a bit. (This recipe should make about 20.) Cook in a skillet oiled with a teaspoon of vegetable oil over moderate heat until done. You'll need to turn once, just as with big burgers.

2. While burgers are cooking, whirl the pineapple and mustard in a blender until pretty smooth.

3. Drain burgers on paper towels. Top with the pineapple sauce. Some sprouts or shredded lettuce are also nice on these burgers. Serve between your favorite whole grain crackers or tiny circles of bread you cut out with an upside-down glass.

A Silly Supper

THUMBELINA BURGERS
WITH PINEAPPLE
MUSTARD SAUCE

◆

ONE-TWO PUNCH

◆

BEASTLY VEGETABLES

◆

SCROOBIOUS PIPPIN CRISP

◆

Whether a casual meal for a few friends or an all-out buffet for a crowd, this menu inspires giggles and guffaws galore.
Use Sunday funnies or a cartoony bedsheet as a tablecloth, along with mismatched plates, cups and utensils. To make Beastly Vegetables, gather raw vegetables, toothpicks and your imagination.
A celery donkey (with fresh parsley for a tail), a lickable lion (carrot curls make a marvelous mane stuck on a mushroom face) and a red pepper ladybug are just a few of the possibilities.

VELVETEEN RABBIT SOUP

MAKES 5 CUPS

Fresh-squeezed orange juice paired with tender, pureed carrots makes a soup as nutritious and lovable as they come. It will warm your soul on a rainy night, though it's tempting served cold, too. Be sure and use fresh-squeezed juice. It makes all the difference in this soup.

PREP TIME: 20 minutes
COOKING TIME: 20-25 minutes

- 2 **lbs. carrots (10-12), scrubbed and grated**
- 2 **cups vegetable stock**
- 4 **tablespoons soy margarine or olive oil**
- 2 **tablespoons chopped fresh parsley**
- 1 **teaspoon tamari or soy sauce**
  dash of sea salt and fresh ground pepper
- 2 **cups fresh-squeezed orange juice**

1. Place grated carrots in a large saucepan with just 1 cup of the stock and margarine. Cover and simmer about 15 minutes, until very tender.
2. When tender, add parsley, soy sauce and the rest of the stock to carrot mixture, and whirl in a blender or processor until fairly smooth. Add salt and pepper.
3. Place mixture back in pan, adding fresh juice. Heat on low until warmed through.
4. Serve warm with a dollop (about 1 tablespoon) of lowfat yogurt, if you like.

PRINCESS PEAS
WITH LEMONADE SAUCE

⇒ 4-6 SERVINGS ⇐

"They could see she was a real princess and no question about it. She had felt one pea all the way through twenty mattresses and twenty more feather beds. Nobody but a princess could be so delicate."

"The Princess & The Pea"
by Hans Christian Andersen

Sugar snap peas are considered the royal essence of the sweet young pea. Not many people can resist them this way—although the sauce works with your garden-variety pea, or even frozen, as well. In fact, this is a delicate and lovely treatment for many a green vegetable.

PREP TIME: 5 minutes
COOKING TIME: 6 minutes

- 1 tablespoon butter or soy margarine
- 1 lb. sugar snap peas, lightly washed and well-drained
- ½ cup Honey Lemonade (page 69)
- chopped fresh mint (optional)

1. Melt butter in a medium-size saucepan. Add lemonade and boil rapidly, uncovered, until the liquid reduces, about 3 minutes.

2. Add peas and simmer for about 3 minutes before serving. Sprinkle with fresh chopped mint if handy.

Dolly's Wedding Day

AESOP'S FABLED CHICKEN

◆

PRINCESS PEAS

◆

MUCHNESS BERRY BISCUITS
(page 61)

◆

CAROB & ORANGE
TRUFFLES

◆

SPARKLING CIDER
WITH FROZEN GRAPES

◆

*Just the thing for that
incredibly special day in
your Dolly's life—this menu
would work wonderfully
for a little girl's birthday
party. Invite best friends
to bring their dolls dressed
in their best. If weather
permits, set up tables and
chairs in the garden. A
favorite floral bedsheet
will make a wonderful
tablecloth. Lots of pretty
ribbons wound around
little baskets of flowers—
and perhaps a few ribbons
hanging from the trees—
should complete the pic-
ture. Play Stevie Wonder's
"Ribbon In The Sky For
Our Love" on your record
player as the lovely couple
march down the aisle.
Have everyone throw a bit
of brown rice.*

SWEET

The night seems to fall a little kindlier on a note of sweetness.
The ticket to these small ecstasies can usually be purchased
with a clean supper plate. Unfortunately, those who fail to finish
those last, plaintive peas cannot expect to partake.
But let us not neglect other hours of the day. There are healthy
sweets here to suit all sorts of occasions, from a sentimental
snack break to the best and brightest birthday parties.
You'll even happen upon a few warm-hearted drinks suited
to sipping while curled up with a beloved picture book.
And now to bed! Lights are out, except for the proud moon that
is shining for you. Pick a passing star to steer by as you set sail
for wondrous lands that lie Far Away and Deep Within. A few
last matters bubble in your mind: Did you tuck in Teddy? Did
you kiss the cook? Did you bid all the children on our blue
planet a taste of peace? Rest well, then. A thousand new
possibilities await you in a treasure chest marked Tomorrow.

DREAMS

TINKER BELL'S RASPBERRY BUNS

≫⊱10 BUNS ⊰≪

Fairies are known far and wide for their talent for inventing sweet buns that are fast and delicious, like this one. They may appear a touch homely, but they're unforgettably spicy and jam packed. Luckily, Tink gave her favorite recipe to the famous English health restaurant and bakery, Cranks, where it is still served today.

PREP TIME: 20-25 minutes
BAKING TIME: 18-20 minutes

- **3** cups whole wheat pastry flour
- **4** teaspoons non-aluminum baking powder*
- **¼** teaspoon cinnamon
- **¼** teaspoon nutmeg
- **4** oz. soy margarine, softened
- **½** cup pure maple granules*
- **⅓** cup raisins
- **1** egg, beaten
- **½** cup lowfat milk
- **4** tablespoons natural raspberry jam

1. Preheat oven to 375°.
2. Mix flour, baking powder and spices in a large bowl. Add the margarine and mix with a wooden spoon until everything's rather crumbly.
3. Stir in maple granules and raisins. Add the beaten egg and milk to form into a firm dough. If you use your hands to do this, it will be easier. (Make sure they're clean and dusted with flour so everything doesn't stick to you.) Form dough into 10 balls about the size of an egg.
4. Space on a lightly greased cookie sheet. Make a small well in the top of each bun with the back of a teaspoon and fill with about a teaspoon of jam. If the dough separates a bit, just pat it back into a nice shape with your fingers. Bake for 18 to 20 minutes, until golden. Cool on a wire rack.

* available in natural food and gourmet stores

"**D**o you believe in fairies? If you believe, clap your hands."
"Peter Pan" by J.M. Barrie

A Little Hint

Sweet spices such as cinnamon, nutmeg, ginger and vanilla are a clever way to help reduce the sugar content of various foods. Their delightful taste and natural sweetness help wake up cakes, pudding, biscuits and many other baked goods. You'll find by experimenting that if you add a bit of these spices, you can diminish the quantity of sugar you use.

THE EMPEROR'S NEW PUDDING

2-3 SERVINGS

There's really nothing to it (except the enchanting taste): yogurt, egg whites and fresh fruit. The Emperor, after he recovered from that little mix-up with his tailors, got into gourmet cooking. This is one of his first creations. These days, you can find him at the oddest hours of the day or night, whipping something up in the cavernous kitchen of his castle. He might even open a restaurant soon.

PREP TIME: 15 minutes
CHILLING TIME: 1 hour

- ½ **pint very ripe strawberries, washed and hulled**
- 2 **tablespoons Honey Lemonade (page 69)**
- ¼ **cup pure maple syrup**
- 4 **oz. plain lowfat yogurt**
- 2 **egg whites at room temperature**

1. Chop strawberries in half and place in a blender or processor with lemonade, maple syrup and yogurt. Puree until fairly smooth. Chill this mixture for about an hour.
2. Using a metal bowl, beat egg whites on high speed until they begin to get stiff and stand up.
3. Fold the egg whites into the strawberry mixture and spoon into little dessert glasses or cups and serve.
4. If you need to make the mixture ahead of time and refrigerate before serving, you'll need to swirl the egg whites back into the puree in each glass a bit, since they'll tend to separate. But you can eliminate the chilling time in Step 1.

Heart's Delight Garden Luncheon

HEARTY SANDWICHES ◆ LITTLE PRINCE LOVE NOTES

MUD PUDDLE DUNK WITH FRESH STRAWBERRIES

BERRY BUBBLE WATER (PAGE 54)

Whether it's Valentine's Day, a treasured Teddy Bear's Birthday or your Mama & Papa's anniversary, serve a luncheon that's full of love. For the Hearty Sandwiches, use the Puss 'n Boots recipe on page 33, but cut with a heart-shaped cutter. A spot beside the rose bushes in the garden is the perfect setting for your table, if that's possible. Lay a lacy cloth or sheet on top, and make red or pink heart placemats from construction paper. Carry through the colors of red or pink and white with whatever's handy in plates, cups and napkins. A vase of roses, tulips, pink and white snapdragons or a pot of narcissus make the mood special if you're indoors. Really, any flower carries a feeling of love with it, whatever the color, so don't be shy about placing a single daisy near each plate, if that's what you happen to have on hand.

LITTLE PRINCE LOVE NOTES

❧ MAKES 2 DOZEN ❧

This is a heateningly quick cookie, made with whole grain cake mix and natural raspberry preserves. It's cut into a heart shape with a cookie cutter after baking, eliminating a lot of rolling time. If you have some on hand on a particularly bumpy day, they will dry a tear or two nicely.

PREP TIME: 15-20 minutes
BAKING TIME: 10-12 minutes

> "If you tame me, then we shall need each other. To me, you will be unique in all the world. To you, I shall be unique in all the world."
>
> **"The Little Prince"**
> **by Antoine de Saint-Exupéry**

½ **cup honey or pure maple syrup**
⅓ **cup soy margarine**
2 **eggs**
¼ **cup skim milk**
1 **teaspoon vanilla**
2 **cups plain whole grain cake mix**
¼ **cup finely chopped pecans (if you like them)**
1 **jar natural raspberry preserves**

1. Preheat oven to 350°.
2. In a medium-size bowl, mix margarine, honey, eggs, milk and vanilla (one at a time, please) until well combined. Stir in the cake mix well and add nuts, if desired.
3. Drop by scant tablespoons onto cookie sheet greased with soy margarine. Flatten slightly with a floury finger or spoon and top each with about ½ teaspoon raspberry preserves. Bake until light gold, 10 to 12 minutes.
4. After cookies cool for several minutes on sheet, take a heart shaped cookie cutter and cut. With metal spatula, transfer to a rack to cool. Enjoy nibbling on the trimmings right now or serve over ice cream later!

QUEEN CELESTE'S CAROB-ORANGE TRUFFLES

❧ MAKES 1½ DOZEN ❧

*These dreamy confections are one way that Queen Celeste—
beloved wife of Babar—keeps her girlish figure. She improved
on that old chocolate and cream indulgence concocted by the
French by relying on some very clever low-fat substitutions
to produce a truffle that is still delightful in every way.
A votre sante! says Celeste.*

PREP TIME: 20 minutes
COOLING TIME: 45 minutes
COOKING TIME: 10 minutes

- ¼ **cup dry milk powder**
- 2 **tablespoons frozen orange juice concentrate**
- 6 **oz. unsweetened carob chips**
- ¼ **cup soy margarine, softened**
- 2 **tablespoons honey or pure maple syrup**
- 2 **tablespoons grated orange rind**
- 2 **tablespoons sifted carob powder or maple granules**

1. In a small saucepan, mix the dry milk with enough water to
form a thick paste—about 2 tablespoons. Add the orange juice
concentrate and carob chips, and cook over medium-low heat,
stirring frequently, until mixture is melted and smooth, about
10 minutes. Remove from heat.
2. Add the softened margarine, orange rind and honey to the
saucepan, stirring to combine. Pour the mixture into a shallow
bowl and refrigerate until firm, about 45 minutes.
3. To form the truffles, scoop up teaspoons of the mixture and
shape into 1-inch balls. Place the carob powder or granules in a
shallow bowl and roll the balls in it, coating them lightly.
4. To store, place in a covered container in the refrigerator, but
remove about half an hour before serving for richest flavor.

*"What's the French
for fiddle-de-dee?"*

**"Alice's Adventures
in Wonderland"
by Lewis Carroll**

Puddle Jumper's Picnic

HANSEL & GRETEL
SANDWICHES
◆
CAROB SOYMILK
◆
FRESH FRUIT ON SKEWERS
◆
SNOWMAN'S FUDGE
◆

*This is great for when it's
been raining all weekend
and the children of the
house are slightly berserk
with boredom. Invite a few
friends over for this easy
indoor picnic, then put on
your raincoats and hats
and go have a visit
with your neighborhood
puddles. Big, small,
shallow, deep—jump for
joy with them all.
Think of what the poet
e. e. cummings said about
the world in spring being
"mud luscious" and
"puddle wonderful."
Of course, you could
always do it on a warm,
sunny day, when there's
not been a puddle in sight
for weeks. Create several
out of big sheets of
construction paper and
have a jumping contest.
Purple puddles, anyone?*

Snowman's Fudge

You can make a delightful fudge by pouring the Mud Puddle Dunk into a pan and freezing it for an hour or so. It's chilly, but it's great. And like your favorite snowman, it will melt if left in the warmth for very long, so you must eat it cold. Think of it as the perfect fudge for a summer's day!

DR. DOLITTLE'S MUD PUDDLE DUNK

≈ MAKES 2 CUPS ≈

This fabulous carob fondue is a treasured recipe in Puddleby-on-the-Marsh, Dolittle's home town. Serve it with strawberries or chunks of banana or apple. You could dunk whole grain cookies or animal crackers in it, too. Take care to heat gently, to avoid burning the carob.

PREP TIME: 5 minutes
COOKING TIME: 10 minutes

  3 tablespoons soy margarine
 10 oz. unsweetened carob chips
 ½ teaspoon grated nutmeg
  1 teaspoon vanilla
 ½ cup pure maple syrup
 ¾ cup lowfat milk

1. Mix all ingredients in the top of a double boiler or heavy saucepan set over another saucepan with hot water in it. Using low heat, stir until the carob chips are melted and the mixture is smooth, about 10 minutes.

2. It's nice to serve this in a fondue pot, to keep it warm, with your dunkers nearby, but it's not absolutely necessary. You could also dunk the strawberries to coat them ahead of time and set on a pretty plate to serve.

LIONS & TIGERS & BEARS, OH MY!

❧ MAKES 18 ❧

These cupcakes make wonderful child-sized birthday cakes, with their wholesome and heavenly maple-peanut smell. Once again, whole grain cake mix makes quick work of the job. After the cupcakes cool, spread with Auntie Em's Famous Fudgy Frosting and stick a lion, tiger or bear from a box of natural animal crackers on top.

PREP TIME: 20 minutes
BAKING TIME: 20-25 minutes

¼ **cup soy margarine, softened**
¾ **cup pure maple syrup**
2 **eggs**
2 **teaspoons vanilla extract**
½ **cup natural peanut butter**
2 **cups plain whole grain cake mix**
½ **teaspoon grated nutmeg**
1 **cup lowfat milk or soymilk**
3 **tablespoons plain lowfat yogurt**
   small box of natural animal crackers

1. Make the frosting first, since it must cool in the fridge a while.
2. Preheat oven to 350°. Grease muffin tin well with vegetable oil or line with foil papers.
3. In a large bowl, gradually add the maple syrup to the softened margarine. Beat in eggs, one at a time. Beat in vanilla and peanut butter. Add cake mix, nutmeg, milk and yogurt (one at a time) and stir until mixed well.
4. Spoon batter into tins or papers, filling about ¾ full. Bake for 20 to 25 minutes, until a toothpick inserted in the center comes out clean. Run a sharp knife around cupcakes and remove from pan right away. Cool on a rack before frosting.

A Little Hint

This cupcake is equally irresistible when made with carob cake mix instead of the plain variety.

AUNTIE EM'S FAMOUS FUDGY FROSTING

❧ MAKES 2 CUPS ❧

Auntie Em has become famous for this frosting, but really she got the idea from Dr. Dolittle the last time he was passing through Kansas. She simply makes his Mud Puddle Dunk (page 81) and lets it cool in the fridge for an hour or so, until it reaches a nice frosting consistency. It's best to frost cupcakes shortly before serving, she suggests.

   Since the cupcakes only need about 1 cup of frosting, you can cut the recipe in half. Then again, you could make the whole batch and turn the rest into Snowman's Fudge (page 81) or carob-coated strawberries.

MARY POPPINS' AMAZING PEACHY PIE

🐧 6 SERVINGS 🐧

It's positively amazing how quickly a bunch of bananas, peach yogurt and fresh blueberries (with a cookie crumb crust as accomplice), turn into a pie that, like Mary Poppins herself, is practically perfect in every way.

PREP TIME: 20 minutes
COOKING TIME: 25 minutes

> 4 tablespoons melted soy margarine
> 2 cups whole grain graham crackers, crushed
> 5 big ripe bananas
> 1 cup natural lowfat peach yogurt
> 1 pint blueberries, washed

1. Preheat oven to 375°.

2. Mix margarine and graham cracker crumbs until they begin to form a ball. Using a fork, press into a 9-inch pie pan, then spread a single layer of blueberries in the bottom, covering the crust completely.

3. In a blender or processor, combine bananas and yogurt until smooth. Pour into crust and bake for about 25 minutes. Turn heat off and leave pie in the oven an extra 10 minutes.

4. Decorate top of pie with more blueberries before serving and a few mint leaves if handy. You'll like this pie served cold as well as warm, by the way.

> **"T**hat sounds like a pie-crust promise—easily made and easily broken."
>
> **"Mary Poppins"**
> **by P. L. Travers**

A Little Hint

This pie is equally practically perfect with a combination of raspberries and raspberry yogurt, peaches and peach yogurt, strawberries and strawberry yogurt, etc., etc., etc. Then again, you could go on forever crisscrossing things: fresh raspberries with lemon yogurt, fresh blueberries with vanilla yogurt, etc., etc., etc. And you haven't even begun to experiment with various whole grain cookies for the crust . . .

BALOO'S MINT BROWNIES

~ 12 BIG OR 24 SMALL BROWNIES ~

Baloo, the wondrously wise old bear in Kipling's two volumes of the "Jungle Book," taught little Mowgli that honey and roots and nuts were just as pleasant to eat as meat. Baloo hoped these light and delightful brownies might help Mowgli feel a bit more brave. And so they did. If you, too, like nuts, by all means throw in a well-chopped handful or two.

PREP TIME: 20 minutes
BAKING TIME: 35-45 minutes

- ⅔ **cup unsweetened carob chips**
- ½ **cup soy margarine**
- ½ **cup honey**
- ½ **cup pure maple syrup**
- 3 **eggs**
- 1½ **teaspoons pure vanilla extract**
- 1½ **teaspoons pure mint extract**
- 1 **cup whole wheat pastry flour**
- ½ **teaspoon baking powder**
- 2-3 **tablespoons carob chips**

1. Preheat oven to 325°. Coat a 9-inch square or a 9- by 13-inch pan (square pan will produce fat brownies) with vegetable oil.
2. In the top of a double boiler set over boiling water, melt carob chips on low heat, taking care not to burn. Set aside to cool.
3. In a large bowl, mix margarine (softened to room temperature) with honey and maple syrup. In a smaller bowl, beat eggs with a mixer until light and fluffy. Add them slowly to the margarine mixture, beating with the mixer.
4. Stir in the vanilla and mint extracts, and then the cooled carob.
5. In a small bowl, mix flour and baking powder, then gently fold into batter.
6. Scrape batter into pan and sprinkle the top with more carob chips. Bake for 35 to 45 minutes, until center is set (the small pan will take longer). Do not overbake. Cool in pan before cutting.

> "So Baloo, the Teacher of the Law, taught him the Wood and Water Laws: how to tell a rotten branch from a sound one: how to speak politely to the wild bees . . . what to say to Mang the Bat when he disturbed him in the branches at mid-day: and how to warn the water-snakes in the pools before he splashed down among them."
>
> **"The Jungle Book"**
> **by Rudyard Kipling**

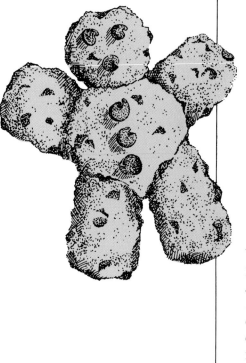

"*I* have many flowers," he said. "But the children are the most beautiful flowers of all."

"The Selfish Giant"
by Oscar Wilde

SELFISH GIANT COOKIES

~MAKES ABOUT 8~

This whole grain cookie is bursting with the taste of peanut butter, maple and cinnamon. It is fashioned rather simply by tiny hands into the shape of a giant and was inspired by Oscar Wilde's lovely story of the giant who learned that it is children who truly make this earth a garden.

PREP TIME: 30 minutes
BAKING TIME: 12 minutes

1 cup canola oil* or melted soy margarine
1 cup maple granules
1 egg
1 cup fresh-ground peanut butter
1 teaspoon pure vanilla extract
1 teaspoon baking soda
1 teaspoon cinnamon
3 cups whole wheat pastry flour
  unsweetened carob chips

1. Preheat oven to 350°. Coat a cookie sheet or two with a bit of oil.
2. In a large mixing bowl, beat all but the last ingredient together, adding one at a time, and mixing well after each addition.
3. You create a giant this way: Put 2 tablespoons of cookie dough on the cookie sheet. This is the body. Put 2 teaspoons of dough on top of this, to create a head. Add another 2 teaspoons for each arm and leg. Flatten each mound a bit with your fingers, taking care to elongate arms and legs. (Wet fingers will stick to the dough less). Take carob chips and add eyes, nose and buttons down the front. If you really like carob chips, stick a few more wherever it pleases you.
4. Make more giants, keeping them at least an inch apart on the cookie sheet. (Feel free to make smaller giants, if you like.)
5. Bake for about 12 minutes. Let cool and remove with a metal spatula.

*These can be made with soy margarine or any natural vegetable oil, but do try them with canola oil, which has the lowest saturated fat content of any vegetable oil. Like peanut oil, it is a monounsaturate—now thought to help protect against the effects of cholesterol in the blood stream. But its delicate aroma is ideal for most baking needs—many people prefer it to safflower or sunflower oil. You'll find it in natural foods stores.

UNCLE SAM'S FRUITFUL SUNDAE

❧ 4-6 SERVINGS ❧

Three cheers for the red, white and blue. This bright berry sauce is quite a sight when drizzled over a bowl of wonderful honey or maple-sweetened vanilla ice cream. It will create many smiles on a summer night.

PREP TIME: 10 minutes

- ½ **cup natural strawberry preserves**
- ½ **cup natural berry juice (choose the brightest red bottle on the shelf)**
- 1 **pint natural vanilla ice cream**
- ½ **cup fresh blueberries, washed**
   sliced fresh strawberries (optional)

1. In small bowl, mix preserves and juice until well combined. Divide ice cream among serving bowls and pour on berry sauce.

2. Add blueberries and strawberries and salute your sundae before it disappears.

A Little Hint

This bright and saucy berry juice and jam concoction for Uncle Sam's sundae has more uses than you can count. It will brighten up a pile of pancakes, pep up a plate of cottage cheese and beautify a bowlful of fresh fruit or plain yogurt. But have you ever tried **Berry Juicy Chicken**? You can marinate chicken in it, or drizzle some of the sauce over the chicken before broiling or baking, or use it to baste chicken you're cooking on the grill.

"**F**rom breakfast on all through the day
At home among my friends I stay;
But every night I go abroad
Afar into the land of nod.

All by myself I have to go,
With none to tell me what to do
All alone beside the streams
And up the mountain-sides of dreams."

"A Child's Garden of Verses"
by Robert Louis Stevenson

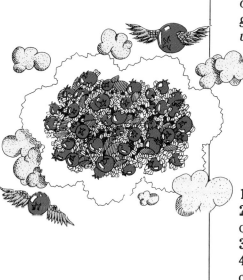

> "Never be mean in anything; never be false; never be cruel."
>
> **"David Copperfield"**
> **by Charles Dickens**

SILVER LINING BLUEBERRY COBBLER

4-6 SERVINGS

If the grill's red hot, this is a summer dessert idea that's almost as easy as toasting marshmallows—and much tastier. You can substitute any favorite summer fruit, such as ripe peaches or other kinds of berries. You can even combine them if you like. But if it's winter, don't grieve. Simply cook the cobbler in a 400° oven for about 25 minutes. Experiment with various kinds of granolas, too. You haven't lived until you've tasted this over vanilla ice cream.

PREP TIME: 10 minutes
COOKING TIME: 20-25 minutes

- 1 **pint blueberries**
- 2 **cups maple nut granola***
- 2 **tablespoons soy margarine, melted**
- 2 **teaspoons Honey Lemonade (page 69)**
- 2 **teaspoons honey or maple syrup**

1. Make a double-thick, 12-inch square of heavy-duty foil.
2. Combine all ingredients in a bowl, place on foil and fold foil over into an airtight package.
3. Place on grill over hot coals for 20 to 25 minutes.
4. When finished, open the top of the foil and cut it with kitchen scissors in a kind of cloud shape—sort of scalloped—and put the foil packet on a plate to take to the table and serve.

*available in natural food stores and supermarket health sections

"The Scroobious Pip went out one day
When the grass was green and the sky was gray.
Then all the beasts in the world came round
When the Scroobious Pip sat down on the ground.
The cat and the dog and the kangaroo,
The sheep and the cow and the guinea pig too,
The wolf he howled, the horse he neighed,
The little pig squeaked, and the donkey brayed,
And when the lion began to roar
There never was heard such a noise before.
And every beast he stood on the tip
Of his toes to look at the Scroobious Pip."

"The Scroobious Pip" by Edward Lear

90

SCROOBIOUS PIPPIN CRISP

❧ 9 SERVINGS ❧

Pippin apples, rolled oats and apple juice team up to make a nice variation of a traditional, and terrifically simple, dish. Serve it with a sparkling apple juice toast to Edward Lear.

PREP TIME: 20 minutes
BAKING TIME: 35 minutes

   2 **cups Pippin apples, washed and thinly sliced**
   2 **tablespoons fresh lemon juice**
   ¼ **cup honey or pure maple syrup**
  1½ **cups rolled oats**
   ½ **cup whole wheat pastry flour**
   ½ **cup safflower oil or melted soy margarine**
   1 **teaspoon cinnamon**
   ½ **cup walnuts, finely chopped (optional)**
   ½ **cup natural apple juice**

1. Preheat oven to 375°. Generously grease a 9-inch square pan with vegetable oil.
2. Spread prepared apples in the bottom of the pan. Cover with lemon juice and then honey.
3. In a medium-size bowl, combine flour, oats, oil, spice and nuts. Spread over apples and pour apple juice on top. You can sprinkle a bit more cinnamon on top.
4. Bake for 35 minutes and serve. This recipe, by the way, is preposterously popular when made with pears, too. Try it with Asian pears, a crossbreed with a pear taste, but a crunchy apple consistency.

A Little Hint

An apple sectioning ring is a handy tool to have on hand. It makes quick slices for this kind of recipe that you can cut in half again by hand for thin slices. It's particularly perfect for when you crave an apple laden with fresh-ground peanut butter—and need it QUICK. Just place the small ring in the middle over top the apple stem and press down continuously until ring cuts all the way through.

SLEEPING BEAUTY

❧ 1 SERVING ❧

Warm, carob-rich milk with a peppermint twist.

PREP TIME: 3 minutes
COOKING TIME: 5 minutes

- 1 **cup lowfat milk**
- 1 **peppermint herb tea bag**
- 1 **teaspoon carob powder**
- 1 **teaspoon honey or maple syrup**

1. Pour milk in small pan, add tea bag and warm over low heat. In a cup, combine the carob powder and honey. When well-blended, add to milk and continue to warm. Remove tea bag before serving.

A Little Hint

This recipe works fine using packaged soymilk— whether plain, vanilla or carob-flavored— in place of the milk. Just eliminate sweetener if you're not using plain soymilk, and eliminate carob if using carob soymilk.

WINKEN, BLINKEN & NOD

❧ 1 SERVING ❧

Since Hans Christian Andersen forgot to leave us the sleep-inducing recipe for what he called "diamond tea" (made mostly with dew), here's an alternative concoction of sweetened warm milk and cinnamon tea, guaranteed to turn anyone into a beautiful dreamer.

PREP TIME: 2 minutes
COOKING TIME: 5 minutes

- 1 **cup whole or lowfat milk**
- 1 **teaspoon honey or pure maple syrup**
- 1 **cinnamon herb tea bag**

1. In a small pan, combine the ingredients and warm over low heat, stirring now and then. Remove tea bag and serve in your favorite mug.

GRATEFUL ACKNOWLEDGEMENTS

While I have often done it in spirit, I here thank in print the authors of the timeless works of children's literature quoted herein. Today, more than ever, it seems a bit like opening a treasure chest to bury one's self in the pages of these books. I drew special inspiration from the everyday heroes of Hans Christian Andersen, and the wordless wonder of Beatrix Potter's creatures.

I am also indebted to the great number of anonymous artists whose creativity graces these pages. While in many cases their work has been combined and edited to create something anew, their spark of long ago still shines beautifully today. My particular tribute goes to the nameless creator of our front cover lion.

◆

I dearly thank Anna Marie Heinz for her vision and devotion to this project. My deepest appreciation also goes to June deBoehmler and Janet Haygood. For their kind help and assistance, I thank Al Feuerstein, Susan Hardee Norris, Janet Bukovinsky, John Mischak, Rosemary Tottoroto, Jay O'Neill and Nicholas Bouyoukas. Here's a toast to the staff of New Hope Communications for their patience in working around this project.

I particularly thank Doug Greene for his help in moving this dream down the road.

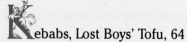

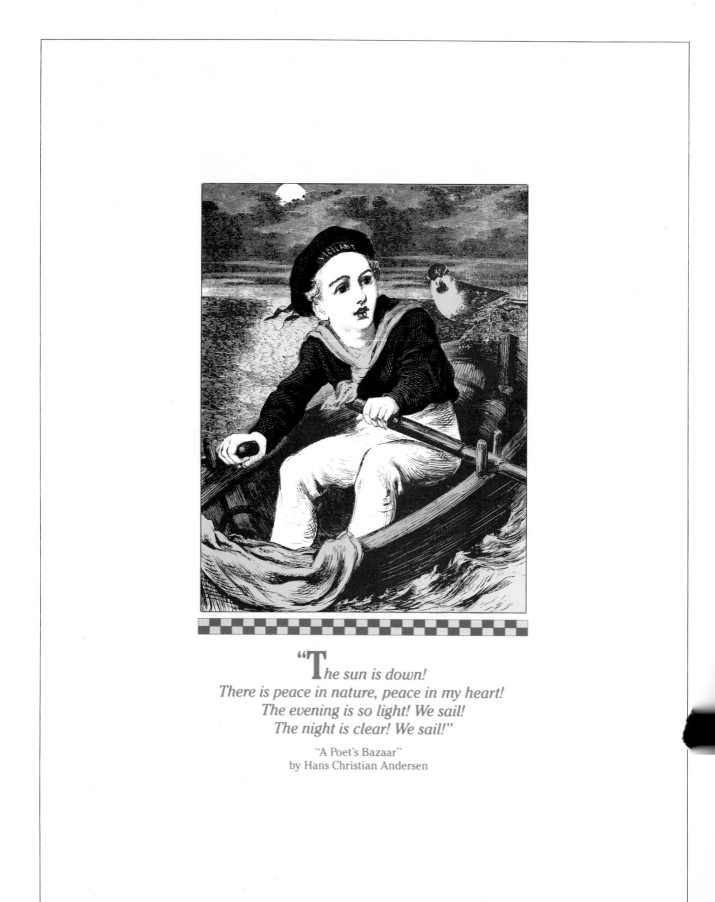

"The sun is down!
There is peace in nature, peace in my heart!
The evening is so light! We sail!
The night is clear! We sail!"

"A Poet's Bazaar"
by Hans Christian Andersen